60-DAY CHRISTIAN DATING DEVOTIONAL

60-DAY
CHRISTIAN
DATING
DEVOTIONAL

PRAYERS AND WISDOM FOR BUILDING A GOD-CENTERED RELATIONSHIP

Sade Curry & Kent Curry

ROCKRIDGE
PRESS

First Rockridge Press trade paperback edition May 2022

Rockridge Press and the Rockridge Press logo are trademarks or registered trademarks of Callisto Media Inc. and/or its affiliates in the United States and other countries and may not be used without written permission.

For general information on our other products and services, please contact our Customer Care Department within the United States at (866) 744-2665, or outside the United States at (510) 253-0500.

Paperback ISBN: 978-1-63807-199-0 | eBook ISBN: 978-1-63807-983-5

Manufactured in the United States of America

Cover Designer: Jane Archer
Interior Designer: Lisa Realmuto and Jane Archer
Art Producer: Megan Baggott
Editor: Chloe Moffett
Production Editor: Rachel Taenzler
Production Manager: David Zapanta

Illustrations © BIBIART/Creative Market

0 1 2 3 4 5 6 7 8 9 10

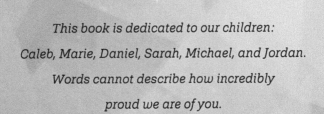

This book is dedicated to our children:

Caleb, Marie, Daniel, Sarah, Michael, and Jordan.

Words cannot describe how incredibly

proud we are of you.

CONTENTS

INTRODUCTION

Picking up a devotional for singles—is this a confirmation of wisdom or a declaration of failure? Does it indicate desperation or the sweet peace of understanding the current season in your life?

Part of the problem is that the word *single* is fraught with so many meanings. Are you:

- New to dating and eager to dive in?

- Jaded by a recent divorce? Feeling old and out of touch?

- Tired of being single your whole life and wondering when it will be your turn?

- Rebuilding confidence after a painful breakup?

- Restarting your life in a new city or situation?

All are considered "single." None are quite alike. Happily, Scripture speaks directly to you in whatever situation you find yourself, and each devotion in this book is structured to highlight the Bible's wisdom for you today.

Popular culture glorifies the single life as if it were all brunches with friends, happy hours with coworkers, and nonstop fun as you meet other fascinating, attractive, and adventurous singles. No one is ever lonely, and no one ever has any cash flow issues. But living the single life with integrity is rarely portrayed on a screen, because it doesn't always create a nonstop highlight reel of laughter. On the other end of the spectrum, singledom doesn't have to be a dreary existence filled with long periods of loneliness and angst. It's more than a painful purgatory where you wait to be saved into the supposed paradise of marriage or partnership.

Being single is a state of living that offers the gifts of focus, space, and the ability to contribute to the world in unique ways. Sometimes it's simply resetting our minds to the opportunities before us. Sometimes it's accepting being single while also pursuing that perfect partner. Sometimes it's navigating this season of time God has given you to heal, learn, and grow so that your next season will bear more fruit. Sometimes it means recognizing that you are fully loved in Christ—whether divorced or single, any gender or orientation—while also recognizing where you need to grow and change spiritually, mentally, and emotionally. This devotional is positioned to help you create awareness of any misconceptions you have around singleness, dating, and relationships.

We've both been there recently. When we found ourselves dating after divorce, we struggled to find Christian material that addressed the changes in the dating scene that we encountered: advances in technology, dating apps, and social media; seismic shifts in social etiquette and dating dynamics; expectations about spiritual maturity, personal growth, and mental health. This little book helps rectify that challenge.

We experienced the common highs and lows: loneliness, break-ups, falling in love too early, falling in love from afar, rejection, getting ghosted, frustrated prayers, and lying in bed alone while wondering whether we would ever find "the One."

Meeting each other was the fruit of grappling with these challenges, learning from our errors, and trying again, armed with new knowledge. Throughout our individual dating journeys, we embraced therapy, coaching, and a deeper reading of the Bible to connect its principles with the reality of what we were facing. We discovered that the Bible has much to say about healthy relationships, evaluating potential partners, healing from rejection and abandonment, and even how social media and dating apps skew our perceptions.

And now that we have reached the end of the dating portion of our own relationship journey, we continue to apply what we've learned to helping others embrace the gifts of singledom while creating opportunities to find love.

The devotions in this book are designed to give you tools, principles, and encouragement from Scripture that can be applied to the contemporary dating landscape. They include the stories of real people in the Bible who grappled with similar human challenges. (Technology advances have not changed innate human behavior.) Each devotion includes a foundation Scripture, a related story built around a Scriptural principle for today's single Christian, and a practical application via prayer, journaling, or specific actions you can take. An open Bible to read alongside this book is highly encouraged. The quotations in this book are taken from the New International Version (NIV), but feel free to use your favorite version.

This 60-day devotional approach gives you the power to follow the devotions numerically or skip around by theme or your current situation. Of course, this devotional is a useful supplement to your walk with God and is not a replacement for therapy or counseling. There is never any shame in seeking professional help.

Best of all, becoming a healthier single makes you a more effective Christian able to navigate the challenges of dating today. That only opens more opportunities for tomorrow.

DEVOTIONS

Single and Purposeful

And we know that in all things God works for the
good of those who love him, who have been
called according to his purpose.
ROMANS 8:28

D o you ever get the feeling that your life hasn't started until you get married? "When are you going to get married?" "Have you met someone yet?" These questions seem to bombard single people everywhere they turn. The implication is that being partnered is the ideal state and singleness is second best. It tempts you to see singleness as a state of limbo. Thinking that "real life" begins after marriage makes meeting someone the only goal of single life.

If you fall for this temptation, you will live this stage of life with blinders on. You will miss the wealth of growth opportunities all around you. You will live a life on hold instead of a life of faithful purpose and creative adventure.

When was the last time you felt fulfilled knowing God has an extraordinary purpose for you? God always intended for you to live a full, luminous life as an example of true love, joy, and faith to those around you. This purpose isn't dependent on your relationship status. It transcends it. God intends for your life's purpose to be worked out through every stage of your life.

Paul confirmed this view when pointing out, "An unmarried man is concerned about the Lord's affairs—how he can please the Lord. But a married man is concerned about the affairs of this world—how he can please his wife—and his interests are divided" (1 Corinthians 7:32–34). According to Paul (and experience), singles have a far shorter household to-do list on any given day. Because of this, they are more able to focus on accomplishing their highest purpose than married Christians. Married Christians live out their purpose in the context of partnership, children, and running households. Single Christians get to do the same in the context of more time and freedom to make independent choices for the kingdom.

It's so much easier to find time to do the things you love and grow your gifts and talents when you are single. Exploring and doing the things you love are also good ways to meet other people who enjoy the same things. What better way to meet compatible potential partners?

Today is a good day to explore the ultimate, extraordinary purpose that God has for you. Do you know what it is? Are you taking action to fulfill it? Maybe your future partner is waiting for you somewhere along that path.

LET'S PRAY

Lord Jesus, open my eyes to see where my growth in You lies today. Give me the clarity and wisdom to recognize the opportunities I have because I'm single and make the most of them today. Help me engage with life with courage and joy instead of sitting on the sidelines until marriage. Amen.

DAY 2

Loving God First

*He answered, "'Love the Lord your God with all your heart
and with all your soul and with all your strength and with
all your mind'; and, 'Love your neighbor as yourself.'"*
LUKE 10:27

The battle was over. David's forces had defeated Absalom's rebels in the forest of Ephraim. Ahimaaz begged to be given the honor of sharing the news of victory with their king, but General Joab chose a Cushite to be his official messenger. Ahimaaz persisted, and finally, the distraction became too great. Joab said, "Run!"

Ahimaaz raced off. It wasn't long before he saw the Cushite in the distance. Soon Ahimaaz was within shouting distance. Finally, he shot past the Cushite, and despite his exhaustion from the pace and distance, Ahimaaz sprinted through the gate and was instantly ushered into the presence of the king. He did it! He beat the Cushite to the king! The king asked for news of the outcome, but Ahimaaz could only speak of the confusion of battle. When the Cushite arrived, he provided the king with Joab's exact report.

Sometimes we can be an Ahimaaz in dating—so single-minded that we forget our mission. Our mission is to maintain a single-minded devotion to God *while* we're dating, not allow God to become our wingman whenever we feel like we need one.

It's easy to nod at this, because we know what our priorities are supposed to be as Christians, but the absolute electricity of matching with someone on a date or an app can jolt the brain into a state of excited frenzy. There's nothing wrong with the excitement—that's how God made us. The challenge is to be mature enough to keep the mission foremost in our minds so we'll have the right message to tell our king.

In fact, God calls us to have a single-minded devotion to Him. Yes, true. Yet what does that look like in real life? Does it mean going off to become a hermit, monk, or nun? If you do that, then you don't have to think about anything but the mysteries of God. That seems solid, doesn't it?

Living a life dedicated to serving God means living a life of integrity while using your personal relationship with God as the guiding principle for your entire life. Guiding principles are different from rules. (Think of this as following the spirit of the law versus the letter of the law.) Principles offer guidance in most situations, whereas laws are specific to certain situations (sexual matters, honesty, loyalty).

We can apply principles and the law to our lives. We can live a joyous life while single and while dating. Creating a romantic partnership becomes part of our bigger purpose instead of a distraction that gets us off course. We can run the dating race like the Cushite, without forgetting whom we represent and what our mission entails.

LET'S REFLECT

Reflect on your personal relationship with God and what it means for you to always be in a relationship of integrity with Him. How does this play out in your life right now? How do you anticipate it will play out when you date? When you are in a committed relationship?

Remember Your Why

Do not quench the Spirit. Do not treat prophecies with
contempt but test them all; hold on to what is good.
1 THESSALONIANS 5:19-21

The wandering Hebrews were again complaining about no food or water and saying God just brought them out of Egypt to die, so God unleashed venomous snakes among them (Numbers 21). The snakes bit and killed many Hebrews. The Hebrews repented quickly once their friends started dying. They wanted the snakes to be taken away. So Moses prayed for the people, and God told him to make a bronze snake and put it on a pole, and if anyone was bitten by the snakes and looked at the bronze snake, they would live. And that's exactly what happened.

Roughly 500 years later, King Hezekiah ascends to the throne of Judah. While clearing out the worship centers to pagan gods, he comes across the bronze serpent of Moses. That's good, right? What an important relic of the great patriarch of Israel! Except the Hebrews were now worshipping and burning incense to it. Hezekiah had it broken into pieces.

At some point, a physical representation of God's grace had become an idol, something they devoted their focus to instead of concentrating on their primary communication with God. This can happen to how we see relationships. They can become idols.

On the journey to find love, it's easy to get caught up in finding your partner, rushing off to the altar to clinch the deal, and completely forgetting why you wanted all of this in the first place. It's possible to want to find love for external reasons—like wanting what everyone else is doing—instead of for clear reasons that matter to you.

What's your reason for wanting a relationship? Is it because it's expected of you by social conditioning? Is it to hopefully end your mother's nagging? Is it to stop being the only single person in your friend group?

What do you really want from life? What will life look like for you the day after the wedding? Are you hoping that being married or coupled will set you up for overall life success and save you from long years of loneliness ahead of you?

Despite appearances, relationships in themselves do not make us happy. Connecting with God and yourself and fully loving and accepting yourself is the true source of happiness. Are you so eager to be in love and love someone else that you haven't slowed down to question what you really want from it?

LET'S REFLECT

Take this opportunity to explore your deeper reasons for wanting a relationship. Make a list without criticizing the reasons. Allow even the nonuseful reasons to come to the surface so you can process them. Adapt the list into the reasons that will hold up for the rest of your life.

No One Is Born with Dating Skills

Praise be to the Lord my Rock, who trains my hands for war, my fingers for battle. He is my loving God and my fortress, my stronghold and my deliverer, my shield, in whom I take refuge, who subdues peoples under me.

PSALM 144:1-2

t's a rare child whose favorite Bible character isn't King David. Little David who killed the gigantic Goliath. Little David who killed the bear and the lion. Little David who became king. Yet in that mythic rise to power—with setbacks along the way—we never stop to realize a simple truth—David had no skills to be king. He had been a shepherd from a small town, a talented musician, and then a rebel on the run with about 600 men.

None of that was enough for him to lead a nation to war and to rule a kingdom. Warriors don't always know how to rule. There were many years between when David was anointed and when he ascended to the throne. It took seven years after Saul's death before he ruled all of Israel. He had two recorded civil wars occur during his reign. Just because he was a "man after [God's] own heart" (Acts 13:22) didn't guarantee a smooth reign. It only reflected his personal walk with God.

David couldn't lean on his shepherd boy skills. He had to learn how to rule, and he had to learn the art of war. He had to learn how to lead strategically and how to properly deal with diplomats and other heads of state.

With the help of a strong commander, dedicated mighty men, and a wise cabinet that included priests and prophets, David eventually won all of his wars to the point that there was peace all around his kingdom.

We are no different from David. We get tossed around in the world of dating because of the assumption that we know how to meet and interact with and connect with other single adults and then choose a life partner with no additional education on the matter. That is a huge assumption.

That assumption makes us feel bad when we don't get it exactly right in the time frame we assume it should take. When dating doesn't go smoothly, we become confused and embarrassed, second-guess ourselves, and feel shame from our mistakes instead of seeing these situations as learning experiences that everyone must go through in some form.

Don't beat yourself up because you think dating should be easier. You may just need to practice your skills. Having trouble meeting new people? Read a book or blog about networking or overcoming social anxiety. Think about hobbies you genuinely enjoy and seek out communities of like-minded people. Having trouble making conversation? Take a communication skills class or practice with friends or family members. Not sure how to decide whom to let go of and whom to move forward with? Talk to a trusted friend, married couple, or spiritual leader to learn more about how to select a partner.

Trust that the Holy Spirit is with you every step of the way as your teacher and counselor.

LET'S PUT IT INTO PRACTICE

Make a list of the trouble spots in your dating journey and look for resources that you could use to learn new skills that could make the process easier.

Day 5

No One Is Born with Relationship Skills

*For the Lord gives wisdom; from his mouth come knowledge
and understanding. He holds success in store for the upright,
he is a shield to those whose walk is blameless, for he guards
the course of the just and protects the way of his faithful ones.*

PROVERBS 2:6–8

Esther was afraid. She had to approach King Xerxes, the ruler of the world's largest empire, in his throne room without an invitation. If Xerxes didn't point his scepter at her, the guards would instantly put her to death.

John Mark was afraid. On their first mission trip, he had bailed on Barnabas and Paul early in their journey because it became so difficult. Now, multiple months later, they were about to embark on another mission trip. He had learned from his mistakes and wanted to go with them again. Asking them to take him back was scary.

Relationships have a way of forcing us to learn new skills if we're determined to keep them alive. That means adjusting some personal tendencies to keep the current relationship growing while also adjusting old habits as situations change.

Change . . . adjustments . . . uncertain outcomes . . . fear. Fear of hard inner work and hurt outer feelings. Fear of diminished love, muddled choices, and bitter arguments. What we rarely fear is the real issue, though—the fear that the love will not continue if we don't adjust together.

Once you meet your person, it can be a splash of cold water in the face to realize that not everything goes smoothly in spite of love and compatibility. It can feel vulnerable to be so open with another person, but without transparency, the relationship will wither for lack of connection. An intimate relationship with another person can be so scary that it actually prevents you from practicing healthy relationship skills.

Beyond dating skills, you will need relationship skills such as assertiveness, building connection, tolerance, resolving differences, forgiveness, accountability and truth telling, the discomfort of saying no, asking for what you want, and vulnerability.

Be open to figuring out what you need to know, not just by talking to family or friends but by reading a book on the topic (your library is full of these books), taking a class, listening to relationship podcasts, and expanding your knowledge on relationships. Don't stay static!

At the root of a reluctance to grow is a sense of fear that change is hard, adjustments are unnecessary, and we can figure it out on our own. The reality is, fear is the fatal internal wound to many relationships that is often covered by outward difficulties. Choose to be Esther or John Mark and face those fears, manage those fears, and overcome those fears in Jesus's name.

LET'S PUT IT INTO PRACTICE

Think of some ways that you can learn the skills required to build a deep connection and healthy relationship with another person beyond the early dating phase. Conversation cards, relationship seminars, and workbooks are a few ideas. Do some research and decide which ones you'd like to try—then start today.

Why Wait for Prince(ss) Charming?

Have I not commanded you? Be strong and courageous.
Do not be afraid; do not be discouraged, for the Lord
your God will be with you wherever you go.
JOSHUA 1:9

You've seen the meme: A picture of a woman on a couch under a caption saying she's ready to date as long as she can stay in the house and wait for Prince Charming to climb through the window to meet her.

We laugh because it's true for everyone on some level. Why do our goals require us to actually take actions? Who designed this system where finding love requires dressing up, going out, feeling awkward, and 48 hours of postmortem overthinking after the date?

When Joshua encourages the children of Israel, his pep talk occurs before they enter the Promised Land, the land of giants and of walled cities, the scary unknown after 40 years in the wilderness. Moses is dead, and now Joshua is the leader. Uncertainty reigns. Inertia is justifiable.

In the same way, dating can look scary. And the horror stories floating out there are no help at all. Logically, you know it's a normal adulting activity, but socially and emotionally, it feels like jumping off a cliff. So you try to figure it all out in advance. Maybe if you plot out all the potential scenarios, you can create safety ahead of time.

But trying to foresee exactly how everything will happen creates premature overwhelm. And being overwhelmed keeps you at a complete standstill that comes from fear and perfectionism—wanting to know every outcome in advance.

But Joshua didn't make any promises of boundless success to the Israelites. He probably wasn't even sure how all these people would cross the River Jordan. All he could do was take the first step in the process of faith, believing that the next right step would reveal itself. He had to leave overthinking and spinning in indecision behind if they were ever going to get into the Promised Land.

Joshua broke his big plan for entering the Promised Land into smaller steps:

1. Send spies ahead to see what they would be facing.

2. Gather the reports on Jericho.

3. Cross the River Jordan into the Promised Land.

4. Ask God for direction in defeating Jericho.

5. Obey God.

Working up the courage to test the uncertain dating market is hard. Your first step can be a small one:

- Download a dating app.

- Find reliable dating resources via podcasts, online videos, or library books.

- Pick out a first-date outfit.

Move forward with confidence, knowing you'll always be moving closer to the Promised Land. Besides, you'll definitely get a funny story or two out of the process. Finally, with every decision, balance fear of the risk in the new against the risk of standing still, as if the world will never change.

LET'S PUT IT INTO PRACTICE

Identify the steps you will take to get started dating. Break them down into even smaller steps. Pick the first one and do it. Then be determined to enjoy the adventure.

Healthy Relationships Part 1: Mutual Reciprocity and Care

Therefore, as God's chosen people, holy and dearly loved, clothe yourselves with compassion, kindness, humility, gentleness and patience. Bear with each other and forgive one another if any of you has a grievance against someone. Forgive as the Lord forgave you. And over all these virtues put on love, which binds them all together in perfect unity. Let the peace of Christ rule in your hearts, since as members of one body you were called to peace. And be thankful.
COLOSSIANS 3:12–15

Your goal in dating is to successfully choose a healthy relationship. But what does the holy grail of a healthy relationship look like? We all know what we think it looks like, but behind the scenes, who knows what's really happening in any relationship? Everyone talks about how much work relationships are. And this is true. But there is a difference between the hard work of a loving couple working out who does which chores and the hard work of keeping a relationship going where there is emotional abuse or physical cruelty.

A couple in a healthy relationship may argue, but their arguments look a lot different from the fights in an abusive marriage or the absence of conflict in a disconnected marriage. Proverbs 10:22 says, "The blessing of the Lord brings wealth, without painful toil for it."

There are some core ingredients that are present in every truly healthy relationship: The partners are mutually respectful and supportive of each other; each partner chooses mature, adult responses to conflict and problem-solving; and there are mutual care and consideration—that is, both partners want the best outcome for the other person. They have empathy for each other's struggles and look out for each other.

In a healthy relationship, both partners should respect each other's physical and emotional boundaries while also sharing their lives honestly and appropriately. They should treat each other with decency and mutual respect no matter what the situation is. Both partners should prioritize the relationship and participate equally in communication and conflict resolution. And when there is conflict, both partners should feel safe with each other, because it is evident that the other will never cause harm.

Honesty is an important core ingredient in relationships. It is critical that each partner's actions match up to their words and there is follow-through on promises made. A healthy partnership also requires each person to be willing to take responsibility for their own actions and make changes when they are wrong.

In a healthy relationship, each person can retain their individuality while also being a part of the couple. The partners each have freedom of authentic expression and can share their thoughts transparently without fear of censure or control. The relationship makes room for each partner to continue to grow and expand the possibilities in their future rather than finding their dreams squashed.

It takes time to verify that the person you are dating exhibits these qualities. Checking in over time for these ingredients can be helpful in making sure you are on track for the relationship you really want.

LET'S PUT IT INTO PRACTICE

Talk to a counselor or spiritual guide about the presence or absence of the core qualities of a healthy relationship in your interactions with romantic partners. Sometimes a second (or third!) pair of eyes will help bring clarity. Always take it seriously if any of these qualities is missing, and reach out for help.

$\mathcal{D}$AY 8

Healthy Relationships Part 2: What Makes Chemistry *Chemistry*?

This is my beloved, this is my friend.
SONG OF SONGS 5:16

I n sports it's called "momentum." In music it's often called "the intangibles." In love it's called "chemistry." Everyone knows the obvious signs of success—winning in sports, top-flight songs in music, and sizzling togetherness. But most important is the magic of the little things within a team, a group, or a couple.

Sometimes external success and the appearance of perfection can mask serious flaws. The team with the most wins in the regular season rarely wins the championship in most sports leagues. Why? Because it is missing the "little things" and "intangibles" that create long-term success.

In a relationship, there are also little signs that can indicate that a relationship goes beyond adrenaline, sexual connection, or a mutual desire to avoid loneliness. These indicators can tip you off that you are participating in a full, healthy relationship that has the potential to overcome life's challenges and last a lifetime.

Some of these little signs include:

Spontaneous, unplanned laughter. When a couple finds themselves sharing spontaneous giggles in a shared moment or an unplanned inside joke or simply laughing at the same observation of the world, it's an indicator of a deeper connection. It represents trust and safety. Scripture confirms this when it shares, "A cheerful heart is good medicine, but a crushed spirit dries up the bones" (Proverbs 17:22).

Appreciation. This is not gratitude or a spirit of thankfulness that God has put this person into your life or for how much they've helped you become a better person. Appreciation is an awareness of your partner's value, a recognition that their talents and abilities not only complement yours but also provide value to the larger community. It is appreciating how they've survived their personal challenges with grace or tenacity despite their flaws. Jesus seemed to have a deep appreciation for Martha, Mary, and Lazarus to the point that He set out to visit them before going into Jerusalem for His final visit (John 11–12). A final time with friends who appreciated Him for who He was and not because of fame or power or connection.

Inspiration and service. A compelling partner fires the need within you to be a better version of yourself. You find yourselves dreaming together about helping others and making the world a better place. The New Testament is rife with exhortations to take care of the widows, the poor, the sick, the prisoners, and the hungry in a direct manner. Giving money is helpful, but personally getting involved brings out the best in all of us and inspires us to be more.

Mutual affection, fondness, and friendship remove any need for competition or tit-for-tat behavior. When there is a real friendship, you are each other's "person," and you find yourselves truly enjoying each other's presence in all situations. Any duo who enjoys these smaller joys will find they are set for a lifetime of joyful partnership.

LET'S PRAY

Lord, please lead me to a love that is full of joy, laughter, and mutual support to take through life, a friendship in which we truly appreciate each other. Give me a relationship that brings refreshment to both of our souls, builds us both up, and provides a haven from life's storms. Amen.

$\mathcal{D}$AY 9

Healthy Relationships Part 3: Building Love, Building Community

God sets the lonely in families, he leads out the prisoners with singing; but the rebellious live in a sun-scorched land.
PSALM 68:6

We humans are social creatures. Pack animals. That's the way God made us. Individually, we relate to our packs in different ways. Whether we are extroverts or introverts, we all play different roles within our communities. You might be a leader in one community, a follower in a different group, and a collaborator in a third circle.

Sometimes we forget that a romantic relationship isn't just for the benefit of the happy couple.

Our world is trending toward the worship of the individual, but the Bible is a series of sacred writings whose themes in nearly every story constantly remind us of the importance of community. Perhaps it is the Jewish community praying together in Esther, or the close-knit brotherhood of Bethlehem keeping Boaz abreast of that attractive Moabite woman now living with Naomi, or the interlocking teachers (Barnabas, Paul, Apollos, Aquila, and Priscilla) connecting the puzzle pieces of the first-century church together throughout the Mediterranean basin. But all of these and more reinforce the importance of a community of believers working together for God's glory.

The key to that community is the building block of the couple. We notice Abraham and Sarah, Moses and Zipporah, or Peter and his wife affecting their communities, but there's also the negative model of Ananias and Sapphira (Acts 5), providing such a powerful example of the wrong type of influence that a married couple can have in a community that Luke felt compelled to include them in the Acts of the Apostles.

Pursuing a romantic relationship is a noble and worthy goal that creates benefits for the two people involved and for the world in general. Biologically, we have a desire to procreate, but healthy romantic relationships go beyond the continuation of the species. They help create healthy communities to minister to and bless the hurting and the vulnerable around us while simultaneously strengthening and encouraging everyone else.

But that means the couple must take on that responsibility and honor as they participate in their community and church. To increase the effectiveness of that couple, each partner can prepare by living a healthy, Christian life beforehand.

You don't get the impression that Aquila and Priscilla suddenly began teaching and tent-making around the Mediterranean without living full lives before they were married. (Indeed, many scholars think she was from a wealthier family and the lead teacher of the two.) Paul wrote that we should be "devoted to one another in love. Honor one another above yourselves" (Romans 12:10).

This means creating a reliable social support system that helps reflect a robust self-image while you're still single. It means laying down the lines of discipline to be successful on your own while seeking a partner. It means seeking to understand yourself well enough so you understand the type of person who will encourage your own path to self-discovery and depth.

LET'S REFLECT

Think about your future relationship beyond just you and your partner. What does community look like for you now? How do you envision your community will look for you in the future? How would your relationship fit into the community and vice versa? Sharing this with the people you date can help you get a sense for compatibility.

$\mathcal{D}$AY 10

I'm Not a Negative Person, Until We Talk about Dating

We demolish arguments and every pretension that sets itself up against the knowledge of God, and we take captive every thought to make it obedient to Christ.
2 CORINTHIANS 10:5

Everyone loves to bash the contemporary dating scene. You've heard all of the horror stories from those who are participating and those who are not. And that doesn't even count all of the family members who've read a horrible story on the internet. It goes something like:

"All the good ones are taken."

"Dating apps are for hookups. No one wants a relationship."

"No one wants to put in the effort."

"They are all emotionally unavailable; it's like picking through the trash."

"You're going to have to take on all their baggage if you get serious."

It's easy to fall into the trap of letting these thoughts direct your journey. You become defensive. You lead with hurt. Even before you go on a date, you assume the other person will be unsuitable.

It's easy to forget that negative thinking is the default mindset for human nature. Yet God calls it unbelief. It might feel helpful to sit around with our friends and rehash the worst stories, but the venting sessions are not as useful as they seem.

Recycling negativity blocks out the fact that the best stories are just as true as the worst. They are just not as interesting to retell. Yet they are exactly what God wants us to focus on. He calls us to faith, to aspire to think and act from a higher plane.

Paul taught the Philippians that they were responsible for choosing what to think about: "Finally, brothers and sisters, whatever is true, whatever is noble, whatever is right, whatever is pure, whatever is lovely, whatever is admirable—if anything is excellent or praiseworthy—think about such things" (Philippians 4:8).

The Bible calls us to choose to see possibilities in God's promises. What you choose to think and believe is the indicator of whether you're partnering with God on your journey or being carried away by the latest dumpster fire scenario on the internet.

When we boldly proclaim God's Word through our actions and move forward in faith, we are saying that what He says is more important than our circumstances. We choose to focus on evidence that good things can happen and that we can expect good even if the current evidence points in the opposite direction.

It is possible to be realistic without being negative. It's true that there are some unsuitable partners out in the world, but undoubtedly, there will be some suitable ones. And it's your choice which story you choose to tell.

"You wouldn't believe the nice person I met over coffee yesterday."

"I've been on a couple of good dates."

"I know some people who met their spouse on a dating app."

"Dating is a challenge, but I'm willing to persevere."

"I can do this."

LET'S PRAY

Lord, change my thinking. In a world that thrives on negativity, I want to reflect the faith and hope You instill in each of us. In a world that maximizes fear, I want to reflect peace and hope. I ask You again to show me how You see each situation so that I think like You. Amen.

$\mathcal{D}$AY 11

Am I Enough? I Am Enough!

But who are you, a human being, to talk back to God? Shall what is formed say to the one who formed it, "Why did you make me like this?"
ROMANS 9:20

66"How did I end up a widow living with my grumpy mother-in-law in her hometown where I know no one?"

"I'm so awkward that my parents are sending a servant to find me a wife I'm supposed to love. There's no way this is going to end well."

"I've got the brains and my looks, but my family is connected to no one. Who's going to want me?"

What if Ruth, Isaac, and Esther all focused on their biggest insecurities? What if they became obsessed with their shortcomings to the point that they refused to notice their strengths and past accomplishments?

Would Ruth have decided she was a homely Moabite in a Bethlehem full of hot Hebrew influencers and given up? Would Isaac have decided there were too many Ishmaels in the gym and he could never measure up, so he should give up? Would Esther have decided she couldn't keep up with the smart girls who went to Shushan Academy and given up?

No. All of them decided that their shortcomings were not a problem for God. All of them decided their assets were enough to attract the right spouse. So Ruth showed spunk and an indisputable work ethic that nabbed Boaz. Isaac played to his strengths to enjoy one of the strongest marriages recorded in Scripture. Esther proved she was not only beautiful but smart, planning with the eunuchs to show off her best for the king.

If we're not careful, we will focus too much on our faults and weaknesses. Our ability to criticize ourselves can be bottomless. This accomplishes nothing and keeps us from living joyously.

It doesn't accomplish anything or help anyone to dwell on your faults. It's also an easy habit when life doesn't go as we'd wish. It is healthier to have a balanced view of yourself. Everyone has both assets and shortcomings. It's just being human. You can't put your best qualities out into the world if you are only focused on what's wrong with yourself.

It's energizing and mature to focus on your strengths at least as frequently as your faults. What you believe about yourself will show up on your dates, so make sure you're familiar with the best of who you are.

LET'S PUT IT INTO PRACTICE

Make a list of your best qualities—past accomplishments, strengths, gifts, and skill sets. Put the list aside for a day, then revisit it and add more items to the list. If this is especially hard, get together with a friend and brainstorm a longer list. Print the list and place it somewhere you can see it daily.

Living in Love Every Day

I have loved you with an everlasting love;
I have drawn you with unfailing kindness.
JEREMIAH 31:3

Once, when talking to my best friend on my mobile phone, I became deeply absorbed in our conversation, as always. We decided to set up a date to meet in person, so I began looking for my phone so I could add the date to my calendar right away. It took quite a few minutes of frantic searching before I realized I was speaking to her on it.

That moment of looking for what I already had was a funny one. However, looking for something we need as deeply as we need love can create pain. When we focus on the absence of romantic love, we create despair by reinforcing the belief that we are unloved and abandoned.

We often refer to our single journey as a "search for love" or "looking for love." These phrases can lead us to believe that love is absent from our lives until we are coupled. Nothing could be further from the truth. Love isn't trapped inside your future mate, unavailable to you until you find them and they "give you love."

We are not without love. God is love, and He makes Himself and His love available to us throughout our lives. Love has many building blocks and facets: the love between parents and children and brothers and sisters, affection shared between best friends, and even the love that we have for awe-inspiring experiences that come our way. All of these are loving gifts that God gives out of His kindness. Each one is a signpost alerting you to how abundant love is in the universe.

Amid empty dating apps or first dates that don't turn into second dates, it is easy to focus on wanting love and not having it yet. But that creates a downward spiral and pulls us away from enjoying life on the way to romantic love.

Instead, we can create fulfillment today by shifting our focus to the unlimited availability of God's abundant love. Decide to live in the love that is available to you today. As you go through your day, look up and around you instead of down. Become aware of what activates love in you. It could be as simple as your cup of coffee or a text from a parent. Pay attention to this love, and allow yourself to focus on it instead of dismissing it or taking it for granted.

No partner can fill your love tank. That power is in your hands. You have the power to live in love every day by connecting with the things you already love. As you go on your dating journey, you can activate the feeling of love by engaging with God's love with heartfelt thankfulness.

LET'S PUT IT INTO PRACTICE

Make a list of what you love. Include people, things, places, and situations that elicit feelings of love, joy, security, and fulfillment in you. Don't worry about your list being shallow or something being unimportant. Focus on making space in your heart to feel the love available to you today.

God Answers Frivolous Prayers

Which of you fathers, if your son asks for a fish, will give
him a snake instead? Or if he asks for an egg, will give him
a scorpion? If you then, though you are evil, know how to
give good gifts to your children, how much more will your
Father in heaven give the Holy Spirit to those who ask him!
LUKE 11:11–13

B eing a Christian is a serious matter: salvation, the kingdom, end times, prayer, sacrifice. This is the stuff we tackle daily. In comparison, getting to a second date with a cute coworker seems frivolous—maybe even foolish.

You wonder whether you'll ever find a partner but are afraid to pray for one because the answer might be no. It feels . . . selfish. So you hide the desire and decide to handle it alone. You act like you don't care whether it ever happens because you're focused on more serious things.

In John 2, Jesus finally moves away from home, gets a bunch of new friends (we call them disciples), and is living His best life on the low-down. No miracles yet. Just feeling the freedom.

Then He ends up at a wedding in Cana in Galilee—and His mom shows up. Ugh. Kind of hard to feel like you're on your own if Mom's nearby. Still, it's all going well; Jesus and the boys are hanging in the corner laughing it up when Mom appears.

"They're out of wine," she says.

Jesus, desperate to look cool in front of His friends, says, "What does that have to do with me? My hour has not yet come."

Mary grabs a servant, points at her number one Son, and says, "Do whatever He tells you."

"Mooooom!" Jesus complains as His friends snicker.

But He humors her and ensures that there is enough wine for the rest of the wedding. And not just any wine, but the best-tasting wine anyone's had until that point.

Great story, right? But isn't ensuring a wedding had enough wine a bit of a frivolous request? The marriage still would've happened if they'd run out of wine. But the family would've been humiliated by the lack of drink, so Jesus saved the day.

Your desire to get married is not frivolous. You should not feel bad about it as you serve a God who wishes to grant your deepest, purest desires.

"Take delight in the Lord, and he will give you the desires of your heart" (Psalm 37:4).

God thinks wanting to be with someone is a good idea. He created marriage, so it's okay for you to declare that you want it, or whatever kind of committed relationship means the most to you. You have permission to mix your prayer for a second date with your prayer for the lost and devotion to the kingdom.

He will listen and answer. Even if He's hanging out in the corner with His dudes.

LET'S PRAY

Father, I know You want to give me the desires of my heart. I would really love to meet my person. I just need a friend and lover whom I can call my own. Thank You for having my best interests and happiness at heart. Amen.

Dream Big, Count Small

Suppose one of you wants to build a tower. Won't you first sit down and estimate the cost to see if you have enough money to complete it? For if you lay the foundation and are not able to finish it, everyone who sees it will ridicule you, saying, "This person began to build and wasn't able to finish."
LUKE 14:28-30

Sometimes it's important to dream big. As long as you've waited, why can't your marriage be a masterpiece?

You want it to be as epic as Michelangelo painting the ceiling of the Sistine Chapel. Yes, we ooh and aah over its beauty today, but he wanted nothing to do with it. Chapel ceilings were painted by second-rate painters—after all, who would even be able to see what you painted up there? Besides, he was a sculptor. (Indeed, the entire time he painted the ceiling, he signed letters to the pope and his family with his name followed by "sculptor.")

Yet, for most of four years, he ended up climbing the scaffolding to the 68-foot ceiling to work in the stuffy air using mostly candles for lighting. The first major panels are impressive, but you can tell Michelangelo's vision of what he could accomplish evolved into something larger, with simpler but more powerful images, after he examined his work from below. The ceiling was declared a masterpiece immediately upon its completion. In a country full of ceiling paintings, there is almost nothing that can compare.

You would love it if others pointed to you and your counterpart as examples of marriage excellence. But any large undertaking requires internal and external work. What exhausted Michelangelo more—the physical task of painting a ceiling on his back or creating a constantly updated vision of beauty in his head to guide his hands? The very process of painting a ceiling changed all the rules of painting—causing him to leave his artistic comfort zone to try to create something that had never before been created on this scale.

So it is when anyone seeks to create a healthy long-term relationship. Jesus told His disciples to be clear-eyed about their plans and projects. What will it take to create your relationship vision? What resources do you need? How much time will it take? What sacrifices need to be made?

Dreams are great, but reality is often a bit more painstaking, and the journey to excellence requires effort. It is hard work to create a long-term healthy relationship that others might classify as a masterpiece.

LET'S PRAY

Father, I have big dreams for my romantic partnership. But I also realize I may have some unrealistic expectations mixed in with an underestimation of what it takes to succeed at relationships. Help me count the cost, cultivate willingness, and show up for the work one day at a time. Amen.

Are You Ready for Love?

*Let us examine our ways and test them,
and let us return to the Lord.*
LAMENTATIONS 3:40

When I (Sade) was 19, I ran for student government in college. I loved campaigning. Meeting people, giving inspiring speeches, and hosting events were fun activities that I enthusiastically participated in.

And I won! It felt great to be elected. But then I got a surprise. I discovered that I hated the day-to-day administrative activities that came with the position. The percentage of people-facing activities was a lot lower than time spent handling paperwork and suffering through meetings. I finished the term, but I didn't run again the next year.

It's possible to be so focused on finding your person that you finally find them and realize that you know very little about being in an ongoing intimate relationship. Finding love is only the beginning.

Next come communication, vulnerability, friendship, and commitment. What happens when your partner makes a joke that goes too far and hurts your feelings? Do you have the skills to have that difficult conversation? Or will you find it easier to walk away?

It's always more tempting to change your partner than to learn to grapple with a new level of growth. But running away only lengthens your journey. On the way to finding love, continue to dig deeper into your own healing and growth.

One easy way to evaluate any gaps in your readiness for long-term love is to look at the fruit of the Spirit. Galatians 5:22–23 informs us that "the fruit of the Spirit is love, joy, peace, forbearance, kindness, goodness, faithfulness, gentleness and self-control."

These are not virtues God will plop into our hearts but attributes we must develop and grow. Some will come harder than others, but all will require development if we're serious about creating a love that will last.

A good relationship will require you to step up to a new level of skill. Commitment requires the courage to start difficult conversations, sacrifice for the other, and demonstrate patience and tolerance. Examine your level of patience, tolerance, and self-control in your current activities and relationships. How are you currently doing with communication, vulnerability, and conflict resolution in your current relationships? Where do you need to strengthen your character, learn new skills, or lean into growth?

If you can't quite trust yourself to assess your skills, ask a friend who will tell you straight up what is true. Go on a growth journey to become as knowledgeable about marriage as you can without being in it. Read some books that go beyond the dating process to discuss committed relationships. Deciding to level up now will reward you later.

LET'S PUT IT INTO PRACTICE

In your journal, write out the list of the fruit of the Spirit. For each attribute of the fruit, write out where you're strong and where you could improve. Brainstorm ways you can improve your areas of weakness, and then seek out appropriate resources that will help you change for love—and thereby make your relationship last.

$\mathcal{D}$AY 16

Sometimes a Good Wing Person Is Just What You Need

Two are better than one, because they have a good return
for their labor: If either of them falls down, one can help
the other up. But pity anyone who falls and has no one
to help them up. Also, if two lie down together, they will
keep warm. But how can one keep warm alone? Though
one may be overpowered, two can defend themselves.
ECCLESIASTES 4:9–12

There's something in our culture that celebrates the brave loner, the uncompromising truth teller: sometimes it's the fearless detective uncovering corruption, other times it's the obsessed Erin Brockovich fighting business chicanery, and other times it's the strong, silent, Clint Eastwood "man on a mission." We love to celebrate heroes who seem to be the strong, silent types.

Scripture takes a different view. In both the Old and New Testaments, the Bible most often celebrates the dynamic duos of belief. In the Old Testament, there are Moses and Joshua, David and Jonathan and then David and Joab, Elijah and Elisha. In the New Testament, Jesus sent the disciples out by twos before the missionary trips were most often in pairs (Barnabas and Paul, Paul and Silas). Yes, there are some prominent exceptions—Abraham; the prophet Daniel for most of his life; Jesus, of course; Phillip ministering to the Samaritans and baptizing the Ethiopian eunuch—but those are the exceptions to prove the rule.

Still, if all of those dynamic duos in Scripture teamed up for greater effectiveness, then perhaps that is a principle worth applying to your dating life. Today, we call the person at our side in relationships a wing person. Once you hit your 20s, it can be difficult to maintain a healthy group of friends. (And you can't count those people on your favorite television series as healthy friends. They're friend substitutes, and the more you have of those types, the greater the warning that you need healthy friends.) After all, friendship is a key building block of healthy love, so creating connection is a good idea before that special someone enters your life.

Take stock of your current friendships. Do you have any close friends? Are you open and vulnerable with your friends and they with you—or is it a one-way relationship? Do you have fun together? Are you making time to connect? Or are the relationships chaotic or confusing? Is your mom the only person outside work whom you talk to every day?

The best wing person is that friend who has your best interests at heart, who will call you out when it's needed, who will properly evaluate those people you'd like to date or who want to date you. Most important, maintaining a healthy friendship means accommodation, joy and laughter, frustration and shutting your mouth when you'd prefer to set them straight, fun, encouragement to draw closer to God, and all the aspects of humanity that prepare you for a mate.

Find your wing person, and create your own dynamic duo. Who knows what doors God might open because of that effort?

LET'S PUT IT INTO PRACTICE

Make a list of single people in your orbit with whom you could nurture a friendship, and ask one of them out for coffee. As you get to know them, ask whether they are willing to be an accountability partner with you on this journey.

Stuck on the Wrong Side of Jordan

*Be strong and courageous. Do not be afraid or terrified
because of them, for the Lord your God goes with
you; he will never leave you nor forsake you.*
DEUTERONOMY 31:6

It was scary for everyone. Moses—the great patriarch, prophet,
and freedom fighter—was dead, and now, after 40 years of
traveling in circles, the children of Israel were ready to fulfill their
mission. It was time to take the Promised Land.

The immediate challenge would be the fortified city of Jericho
on the west side of the Jordan River, but if they conquered the
city—and that was a big "if"—then they were entering a region of
giants that would need to be conquered. Plus, two and a half of the
12 tribes loved the land on the east side of the Jordan so much that
they wanted to settle there. But this was the moment they had been
waiting for. And . . . it was a little scary. Talking about God's promises
and fulfilling God's promises take two very different mindsets. Even
with the miracle of the Ark of the Covenant parting the River Jordan,
there was no guarantee of victory.

Joshua, spy extraordinaire, former top lieutenant to Moses, and
current leader, had to be telling himself to be of good courage even
as he told everyone the same. Suddenly, that part about escaping
Pharaoh and crossing the Red Sea seemed so easy. Sometimes
we must be of good courage when we're on the wrong side of the
dating river. Sometimes the circumstances stay uneven, and any
new prospects seem sketchy.

The metaphoric Jordan River appears to all of us at a different point:

- For some, it's getting on a dating app.

- For some, it's realizing you can stay in touch with multiple romantic partners without misleading them.

- For some, it's asking someone out.

- For some, it's saying no to an offer, which means loneliness instead of mediocre companionship.

- For some, it's going exclusive.

All of these can be challenging and scary. It can be extremely uncomfortable to take action in the moment. It's the Joshua moment of bravery.

This is the bravery that requires valuing the goal and the proposed end result over any temporary discomfort you might be feeling. There are all sorts of reactions to this discomfort: Anxiety is normal. Second-guessing yourself is normal. Overthinking is normal. Wanting to back out is normal. The children of Israel felt all this and more as they contemplated the Promised Land from the other side of Jordan.

But no one makes an impact until they cross their Jordan. Their life remains half-changed. Their dreams remain unfulfilled. They don't reach the point they said they've always wanted to reach. If we are to accomplish a big goal like connecting with that special person and creating an extraordinary relationship, some big, scary leaps will be required. Just take a deep breath and do it.

LET'S PUT IT INTO PRACTICE

Time to play the kids' game where friends dared you to do something scary. Make a list of 10 scary dating actions that you want to take to create dating momentum. Now dare yourself to do one a day for the next 10 days. Ask a friend to hold you accountable.

DAY 18

How Many Fish in the Sea?

*When he had finished speaking, he said to Simon, "Put out
into deep water, and let down the nets for a catch." Simon
answered, "Master, we've worked hard all night and haven't
caught anything. But because you say so, I will let down the
nets." When they had done so, they caught such a large number
of fish that their nets began to break. So they signaled their
partners in the other boat to come and help them, and they
came and filled both boats so full that they began to sink.*
LUKE 5:4-7

You had a week of warm, funny, and flirty text conversations.
Long hours on the phone for another week. You scheduled a
date. You took a leap, showed up, and got stood up.

Ouch. "Never! Never going to do this again. I knew it
wouldn't work."

When humiliation happens, the sting of it burns your cheeks;
your skin crawls with the cringe that makes you want to hide at
home and never, ever step out again.

This is why Simon argued with Jesus. Remember, Simon, Peter,
Andrew, James, and John were all professional fishermen. They knew
what it was like to try different spots in the Sea of Galilee—the fish are
always in this spot at this time of night! Why can't we catch anything?
Let's try a different spot we know works. Look, other fishermen are
over there. Let's go where they are! All night. Nothing to show for it
except the shame and disappointment of full-blown failure.

You might be thinking, "What is wrong with me? I thought I knew
what I was doing. I obviously don't. Don't ask me to do it again,
Jesus. I can't handle doing it one. More. Time. I've already failed too

many times to count. I'll settle for being a failed fisherman." It can be exhausting to keep trying. Rejection is painful and personal. It feels like your heart can only take so much.

Except Jesus said to try again. So Simon and the other fishermen tried again. And they were amazed at the tonnage of fish that appeared in their nets. So much that their boats began to sink. When you connect with the person God wants to give you, the reward will be more than worth the effort.

There may be many empty nets until then. As Jesus made clear to Peter, don't internalize the failure or the shame—you're not a failure even if you failed. You just haven't reached your goal yet. The story you tell at the end will be even better now.

No one in Scripture had a trouble-free life. Everyone suffered pain, failure, and humiliation—but they persevered. And that means you'll capture the big fish at the end.

You just have to try one. More. Time.

LET'S REFLECT

On your dating journey, there will be some setbacks, obstacles, and failures. They will elicit painful emotions. Journal about a dating failure you've experienced. What emotions did you experience? Try to externalize the experience to reduce the sting. How would you encourage a friend in that situation? Then apply that encouragement to yourself.

Taking Leaps of Faith

For the Spirit God gave us does not make us timid,
but gives us power, love and self-discipline.
2 TIMOTHY 1:7

There are basically two types of kids at the pool in summertime: There's the kid who spends an hour tiptoeing into the water and only has 15 minutes to swim. This was me. (Actually, this is still me.) Then there's the other kid who dives right in and gets over the shock of the cold water. Yeah, I hate that second kid, too.

There's an adult version of this: You're so afraid to start dating because of all the stories you've heard and the scenarios you imagine. Instead of getting out there to meet people at coffee dates and parties, you're trying to plan out your journey so that you never have to make a mistake or encounter an uncomfortable situation or feel the cold water of rejection. You're reluctant to experience dates that are awkward and conversations with long silences.

Afraid of having to say no when the most boring person in the world asks to see you again. Afraid you'll find out the picture on the dating app isn't the person sitting across from you. Afraid of being weird in front of a stranger or laughing at the wrong point in a sad story.

It's completely understandable. And unnecessary. Running from discomfort is a poor way to make decisions.

No one in Scripture was immune to making decisions under duress—Mary was a pregnant virgin. Elijah was a fire-breathing prophet running for his life. Paul preached the gospel between stonings, shipwrecks, and snake bites.

Jesus never gave His disciples a pass just because there would be difficult times—indeed, He told them, "Blessed are you when people insult you, persecute you and falsely say all kinds of evil against you because of me" (Matthew 5:11).

We have a natural fear of difficulty. But the reward for enduring hardship is well worth it. Become willing to experience discomfort in texting people who may turn out to be disappointing matches. Be willing to experience failed first dates riddled with clumsy pauses. Be willing to risk the possibility that you might spill a drink all over your date or be stuck with someone who expects you to pay for the meal and "Yes, of course I'd like dessert."

Like every epic undertaking, dating is messy. Creating a bountiful harvest requires getting some dirt on your hands. So get rid of the kid gloves. Jump in with both feet and trust that you can handle whatever comes. God is there to support and hold you through the process—and the process includes the cold water of discomfort. Getting over the shock quickly creates the time and space to enjoy the adventure.

LET'S PRAY

Lord, I don't know why I can face challenges in other areas but dating makes me want to run in the opposite direction. I am ready to be brave and face the challenges of the dating journey. Help me give up reasons to avoid discomfort and look to You for strength instead. Amen.

Lonely or Alone?

Turn to me and be gracious to me, for I am lonely and afflicted.
PSALM 25:16

What's worse—a disastrous date or not even getting enough interest from others to have a disastrous date? Every journey has dull periods when nothing happens. When you go to bed alone and you don't know when the long nights will end.

Looking at social media can create the perception that everyone is part of a happy couple out there living their doubly blessed best life. It's nice when they post their anniversaries with the "We've been together seven years" slogans, but sometimes it feels like they're highlighting what you don't have.

This can be the hardest part of dating. When you shrivel up inside every time someone asks, "So, are you dating anyone?" and it's the same answer you gave last time. Loneliness will occur on the journey. It's normal and part of the human experience. Everyone hates it. No one wants to experience it and be told, "It happens to everyone." But that doesn't change the hard truth—you're alone, and it feels painful.

But being alone doesn't have to create the pain of loneliness. Loneliness is an emotion created by an interpretation of the state of being alone. That seems obvious, but if you are thinking that being alone means you will be alone forever, you're not good enough, and nobody wants you, it creates a painful loneliness that sucks the life out of this season.

On some days, you will long to share a particular activity or thought with someone who understands you and enjoys the same things. But they're not in your life yet. And that thought will make being alone especially unbearable.

In that moment, you can choose a different interpretation of being alone: that it is a temporary state. "I haven't met my person yet, and that's okay." Thinking in this way empowers you to spend this time not in pain or despair but in acceptance, patience, and hope.

Moses and Zipporah were alone, Jacob and Rebekah were alone, Ruth and Boaz were alone, and there was a lot more to all their lives than their aloneness. Purpose brought them together, and Jacob, Rebekah, Ruth, and Boaz became part of Jesus's genealogy.

We can also follow Jesus's example of embracing time alone—He withdrew to a quiet place to replenish Himself, often with a period of prayer included. If alone time is painful for you, it may be an indicator that you need more spiritual growth or need to work through something painful from your past.

Being alone is required for a while, but what you do with that time is up to you.

LET'S PUT IT INTO PRACTICE

Journal on the opportunities that being alone offers you. Ask couples around you what they wish they had done: what opportunities they wish they had taken advantage of while single. What past baggage might have been healed instead of ignored. Ask happily single people what they invest their time and energy in that makes them happy. Take it all to heart and see whether you can take advantage of these opportunities.

Playing the Waiting Game

I make known the end from the beginning, from ancient times, what is still to come. I say, "My purpose will stand, and I will do all that I please."
ISAIAH 46:10

s there a more cinematic and romantic meeting in Scripture than when Isaac spies Rebekah for the first time? It is evening. A mature Isaac is walking into a field for prayer and meditation. Apparently, this is his routine at the end of every day.

Except this time, in the distance is a caravan bringing the wife he has never seen before to him. (Scripture isn't specific, but we'll place the setting sun behind the camels so that they're outlined dark against the orange circle of Sol.) As he spies her from a distance, she looks up and notices him, rugged, only his torso appearing above the grain in the field. Instantly she dismounts her camel and asks Eliezer, the servant of Abraham, "Who is that man in the field coming to meet us?" (Genesis 24:65). "Your husband," comes the reply. Rebekah, despite being described as "beautiful" (Genesis 24:16), covers herself with a veil, as custom demands, before they meet. They are married soon after.

Sigh

Does it help to know that many scholars believe Isaac was 40 at this moment? That Rebekah didn't even know he existed until a third party—Eliezer—met her and said, "I know the perfect guy for you"? But before that, Rebekah had to prove herself to him via the most unusual test in Scripture—by providing water for Eliezer's caravan full of dehydrated camels.

God's life plan is different for everyone. You may have been on your dating journey longer than you prefer. Perhaps you had high hopes for past relationships that faded or fizzled. Perhaps the dating apps have been a desert of viable candidates. None of that means God's plan isn't playing out in your life. Perhaps He is giving you time to heal from past hurts. Or time to develop skills to complete a dream. Or perhaps it's to learn that patience is also an action.

As for both Isaac and Rebekah, physically far from each other while single, trusting God's plan in your romantic life might mean the plan requires an unusual route to make it happen. Different from anyone else's you may have heard of. But isn't that what you'd prefer?

It's important to remember that God knows the end from the beginning. He also sets up the plan from the beginning to the end. Are you willing to trust that plan?

LET'S PRAY

Lord, whether I feel like it or not, I know I am perfectly within Your plan. While I am in neither the beginning stage nor the end, I trust in You. I will use this season of Isaac waiting for his Rebekah. I know You will stay beside me. Amen.

$\mathcal{D}$AY 22

Envy, Jealousy, and Self-Pity! Oh My!

A heart at peace gives life to the body,
but envy rots the bones.
PROVERBS 14:30

Have you ever looked at a couple on social media or in a restaurant or while you're running in the park and asked yourself, "How did they end up with a person as amazing as that?" Or do you compare yourself to others and wonder why a person who is "less than" you could seemingly effortlessly find an amazing partner? Or there's that person who discards amazing people to move on to other amazing people. And you think, "I can't even get someone to look at me, much less schedule a coffee date."

Everyone knows that comparing yourself to others is an extremely harmful way of thinking. It fosters envy, jealousy, and self-pity within you like brain cancer. Envy stains your soul by wanting what they have. Jealousy poisons your heart by fearing you're losing something—status, friendships, opportunities—by their gain. Self-pity locks your mind in victim mode. You feel entitled to what others have. You think you deserve it more than they do. All of these poisons take you out of the driver's seat of your own life. God wants you to ride shotgun in His Lamborghini of your own love story, but you're choosing to be the passenger and observer on everyone else's bus.

This was a challenge in the Bible as well.

Rachel knew envy well. First, she got tricked out of marrying her beloved until her father married her sister Leah to a drunken Jacob.

(How could anyone not feel anger and self-pity over being betrayed by both their father and sister?) Then Rachel envied how easy it was for Leah to have babies while Rachel herself was barren. At one point, Leah traded herbs to bargain with Rachel for sexual access to Jacob—and she even had another son out of that one night (Genesis 30:14–17)! Meanwhile, Rachel stayed barren. She was jealous of losing her husband to someone more fruitful, especially when she was the only wife Jacob wanted.

Envy, jealousy, and self-pity are all on the normal spectrum of emotions, but it can still be hard to own up to the fact that we can nest such vices about other people in our spirit. They all create real damage to our own heart, mindset, and outlook, because stories that could inspire you become weapons for you to use to beat yourself down.

It's important to recognize when you feel envy and take responsibility for it. Be open about it to God. Pray to clear the air. Recognize and admit to your envy, jealousy, and self-pity. Then ask God to plant hope and peace in their place.

And next time you see happy couples on social media, don't use their happiness as a weapon to discourage yourself. Instead, use their story as inspiration and an example of what is possible for you.

LET'S PRAY

Lord, I trust You to write my love story. But my human emotions sometimes get the better of me. Heal the fears and insecurities that cause me to envy others. Help me hold fast to the peace and calm that Your promises bring. Amen.

Whose Voice Are You Listening To?

See to it that no one takes you captive through hollow and deceptive philosophy, which depends on human tradition and the elemental spiritual forces of this world rather than on Christ.
COLOSSIANS 2:8

66 "Don't text first!"

"Wait two days to reply."

"Take a week off for every month you were together before the breakup."

"Make him pay every time."

"Don't pay for her meal every time!"

Pop culture and social conditioning have a lot to say about how to date, whom to date, and what rules to follow to keep the games in play. Some experts say one thing about dating while other experts say the opposite. There's conventional wisdom at church, conventional wisdom within your family, conventional wisdom among your friends, and conventional wisdom on the social media accounts you follow.

Many of these get passed down and tweaked until they just become part of the air we breathe. If you're not careful, you don't even question them, because it feels like everyone believes them. You may find yourself acting out these thoughts and ideas in your dating journey.

Paul was warning the Colossians against the dangers of conventional social wisdom. He wanted them to take the time to question what everyone took for granted and make sure they were learning from Christ and not the world.

He wanted them to lean on God's higher wisdom, because with God there are no rules or formulas. He leads each individual on a unique walk that only they should take. Elijah mentored Elisha. Both were prophets who roamed the same region, yet one was a fire-breathing truth teller and the other a (mostly) kind guide to a healing people. John and Peter appear to have been paired up more than once throughout their ministries, yet one didn't start thinking until he was already speaking, and the other didn't seem to talk unless he was sure he had something to say.

God has a special direction for you as well, but if you're paying more attention to the cultural rules, you'll miss out on your own special path. Yes, you're unlikely to hear an audible voice, but you're likely to feel the rhythms of Scripture come alive in your life in this area when you read God's Word and pray for direction and discernment. It sounds hard, but it's just about keeping a clean heart. That still, small voice Elijah heard long ago is alive and well, listening to your cries and whispering a way to walk in unusual integrity, down a path that only you can see but that perfectly intersects with your future spouse.

It all starts with a choice to listen to the Creator instead of the creatures, the Maker and not the made. It's an easy choice when we stop and listen.

LET'S REFLECT

What conventional "rules" have you been following on your dating journey? Where did the rules come from? Are they helping you or creating confusing results? It's okay to question what you see others doing on their dating journey, pray about it, and make a decision about what works for you.

DAY 24

Will the Real You
Please Stand Up?

*Am I now trying to win the approval of human beings, or of
God? Or am I trying to please people? If I were still trying
to please people, I would not be a servant of Christ.*
GALATIANS 1:10

t's one of the best-known stories in all of Scripture—Isaac was
old and nearly blind. He needed to offer a blessing to the next
generation. Esau was the older twin and due the majority of the
blessings. He was red-haired and hairy all over. The perfect hunter
and outdoorsman. Esau was his dad's favorite who spent a tre-
mendous amount of time hunting on his own, often bringing back
game that fed the family. Jacob, the younger twin, was a mama's
boy who stayed close to home, apparently hairless and smaller
than his brother, with a higher voice. Plus, he was already known as
a deceiver. So while Esau was out hunting for a celebratory dinner
before the blessing, Mama killed a goat, made a meal that tasted
like Esau's, used the goat hair to cover Jacob's skin to make it hairy,
and then sent Jacob in to his father to claim the blessing while Esau
still hunted. A suspicious Isaac ended up giving Jacob the family
blessing, an advantage that remained with Jacob the rest of his life
and was passed on to his sons.

We all cluck our tongues at Jacob's deceitful ways. Except sometimes we change who we are to get a date or while we're on a date
in hopes that we will be what the other person is seeking. After all,
if we act like we're someone else, then that might get us prioritized.
Making small modifications to our personality or our dating profile

or how we act in public to receive that extra attention, that reward, that love can make it an easy price to pay. We can smooth over the "tiny inconsistencies" later.

And yet we forget that Jacob was plagued with deceiving and being deceived his entire life. He dueled with his uncle Laban in deceit and believed his favorite son, Joseph, was dead because he was deceived by his other sons. Then those boys were deceived by Joseph in Egypt. And those were the major incidents of deceit Scripture records.

Once we remodel our personality to fit the perceptions of others, the small compromises get easier. Soon, we can start focusing on the short-term wins (dates with certain types of people who could take you to exciting places you've never been before) instead of the best long-term goals (finding your best counterpart). That's not counting the small compromises in character, the little lies needed to keep the tiny inconsistencies consistent, and the willingness to play games instead of maintaining our integrity through this dating process.

To avoid the fate of Jacob in your own life, make the commitment to live your life with authentic expression. Yes, when you choose authenticity, you will prevent the deeper wounds that self-imposed adjustments will carve into your soul. Best of all, when you connect with the right person, you will have a foundation of honesty and integrity to build on.

LET'S PRAY

Lord, help me live out fully and brightly as the person You have created me to be. Give me the faith to trust that You will bring me to the right person and the right relationship, and teach me that I do not have to play any games when dating. Amen.

Dating like the Apostle Peter (That's Not a Good Thing)

It is a trap to dedicate something rashly and
only later to consider one's vows.
PROVERBS 20:25

The Apostle Peter must have driven Jesus crazy. As if he was that talented child who couldn't stop creating trouble for the master because he cared so much. In every Gospel, Peter exhibited the total confidence of an impetuous, cocky twelve-year-old who thinks they know exactly how the world works.

For instance, from Matthew 26:31–35:

"Someday soon I will be seized by the chief priests and others, who will kill me, but I will be raised back to life on the third day," Jesus prophesies.

"That's crazy, Jesus! That will never happen," Peter proclaims.

"All of you will fall away from me this very night," says a somber Jesus.

"What a ridiculous statement! Though everyone else falls away from you, I will never deny you, Jesus," Peter scoffs.

"Tonight you will deny me three times," Jesus replies.

"I will die before I deny!" Peter insists.

A mob comes for Jesus in the Garden of Gethsemane. Peter draws a sword and swipes off the ear of a nearby servant.

That night, while the Sanhedrin decides the fate of Christ, Peter denies Christ three times in the courtyard.

While some people lean toward self-doubt when dating, there are others who exhibit overconfidence and impulsivity. Perhaps it is fueled by a desirable talent or good looks or an especially valuable piece of property (be it a home or vehicle or boat) or even hidden insecurity. Yet these people recklessly dive into the dating pool, confident that their perfect person is instantly waiting for them.

Often they just want to get the search over and done with and be in a couple. It's a blast posting those pictures together on social media rather than wading through the morass of swipe rights while using exacting criteria that make the entire process go slower. Go with your gut! After all, that works in fantasy football and lottery numbers. Plus, there's the high of rolling the dice to win it all.

Yet we can be as reckless as the Apostle Peter in the dating process. Despite how many times Jesus rebuked Peter, there is no sign he ever took any of those responses to heart. "I'm still right," he seemed to think. "I have a good heart!" He took his one win—"Hey! No one else walked on water"—and pretended that applied to every situation.

We can do the same with each swipe right. We can ignore our values instead of implementing a deliberate, wise search that prioritizes integrity over the cheap highs of every time thinking, "This could be the one!"

After denying Christ, Peter learned to become more deliberate. He acted with confidence when it was appropriate but stopped popping off just because he could. Likewise, we can temper our impetuous "roll the dice" desires by deciding beforehand what criteria make us a deliberate, judicious dater.

LET'S PUT IT INTO PRACTICE

Spend some time evaluating your dating journey up to this point. Make a list of dates and matches so far. When have you held back from self-doubt? When have you rushed forward overconfidently and impulsively? Which is your frequent pattern? What changes do you need to make?

Eyes Wide Open

*By their fruit you will recognize them. Do people pick grapes
from thornbushes, or figs from thistles? Likewise, every
good tree bears good fruit, but a bad tree bears bad fruit.
A good tree cannot bear bad fruit, and a bad tree cannot bear
good fruit. . . . Thus, by their fruit you will recognize them.*
MATTHEW 7:16–18, 20

Sometimes it's good to be the prince. Especially when you're the "Sexiest Man Alive in Ancient Israel" (2 Samuel 14:25), wily, and have 50 young men run before you when you drive your chariot through Jerusalem at a slow pace so everyone can admire your dashing élan. Absalom was admired by all. Even though he was King David's third son, many saw Absalom as the inevitable heir apparent to the throne.

However, Absalom began undermining David's position as king, and soon enough, he initiated a civil war. David didn't want to see it. Even as David's forces left for battle against the rebels, the king exhorted his commanders not to harm his son, putting the kingdom in continued danger. In spite of the obvious evidence that pointed to Absalom's dangerous actions, David allowed his love for his son to cloud his judgment.

Sadly, this seems to be a universal human weakness. When we're in love, we're often in denial. We will overlook harmful behavior and deal breakers in the pursuit of love. Or, once we are with someone, the thought of breaking up and being single again—no matter how legitimate—can be unbearable. We thought this was "the One," and a breakup will create embarrassment with all of the questions from friends and family members. Besides, there were some good times, so we make excuses and hope for the best.

In every situation, but especially in love, we must allow ourselves to see the person in front of us. Their actions tell us who they actually are.

Be slow to trust. Recognize the red flags and deal breakers, and refuse to compromise. Don't make assumptions or explain away your partner's behavior. Ask clarifying questions. Don't just get angry at their actions without holding them accountable, like David did.

Be sure to date in person, not just online. Avoid secret relationships that don't allow your friends' perspectives for clarity. After some relationship stability, make sure your person interacts with your family and friends (via double dates, hangouts, parties, and church events). Integrate them into your current life so you see how they behave in the real world.

Keeping your eyes open doesn't make you picky or judgmental. It means you value your future, your romantic partnership, and yourself. It means you are willing to see behavior you don't want to tolerate for a lifetime. Singlehood is fun compared to a miserable marriage. But a miserable marriage always starts with denial.

LET'S REFLECT

Think about any areas where you might be avoiding the truth of what's happening in your dating life. Are you ignoring any red flags or relationship patterns? Are you minimizing any difficult truths and pretending things will be okay? Write them down and process them.

Judge Not, but Discern Much

Dear friends, do not believe every spirit, but test the spirits
to see whether they are from God, because many
false prophets have gone out into the world.
1 JOHN 4:1

T he survivors straggled over the hill in old clothes and patched sandals, with torn wineskins and moldy bread. "We have come from a far country and only now have arrived after a long journey," they said. "This bread was fresh and hot when we left. Our clothes and sandals were brand new, but look at their pitiful condition today. Please make a peace treaty with us."

Joshua and the rulers of the congregation swore peace to them. Neither Joshua nor the rulers asked counsel of the Lord (Joshua 9:14). In three days' march, they found the land of the Gibeonites. Enemies they were now "at peace" with. They had been tricked. If only Joshua and his leaders had asked the Lord for discernment instead of believing their eyes.

Discernment sounds very heavy, but it's especially important when you're dating.

When you're dating, you meet a lot of people. The book of Proverbs describes people as wise, foolish, simple, and even wicked. There's a good chance you will run into some or all of these types of people at your coffee connections, on dating apps, and at your local church.

God expects you to use His criteria to sort the people you date and not be naive.

It can feel mean to assess whether the other person is a good fit, but wise dating requires you to evaluate others. You need to make a decision about whether a person is right for you. Seeing people for who they are is not judging. Judging is when you put people down to elevate yourself. Judging is pointing out others' flaws while ignoring or hiding your own.

Discernment is different. Discernment is simply refusing to make a final judgment—good or bad—until you have all the information you need. Your feelings and the words of the other person are not enough to create complete clarity. It's important to God to give you discernment and sound judgment. For example:

Don't jump to conclusions because this person checks your boxes.

Refuse fearful thoughts like "Is this the axe murderer loose in my city?"

Refuse presumptive thoughts: "It's only been three weeks, but I feel like I've known them forever!"

"The Lord does not look at the things people look at. People look at the outward appearance, but the Lord looks at the heart" (1 Samuel 16:7).

God knows what is really happening under the surface with the people you date. Let time, patience, and God's guidance show you what He sees. God saw the truth of the Gibeonites, except Joshua forgot to ask.

LET'S PRAY

Father, I am ill-equipped to properly discern the hearts and intents of others. I do not have enough wisdom to recognize future pitfalls and problems arising from me choosing a person I'm just meeting. I ask that You guide me in whom I should pursue and whom I should deny. Amen.

DAY 28

Sometimes You Have
to Walk Away

There will be terrible times in the last days. People will be
lovers of themselves, lovers of money, boastful, proud,
abusive, disobedient to their parents, ungrateful, unholy,
without love, unforgiving, slanderous, without self-control,
brutal, not lovers of the good, treacherous, rash, conceited,
lovers of pleasure rather than lovers of God—having
a form of godliness but denying its power.
Have nothing to do with such people.
2 TIMOTHY 3:1-5

Sometimes there comes that shocking moment when you find yourself dating someone who is not good for you. It's not apparent at first, but as time goes on, you might find yourself on the other side of cruel, mocking words, as David did from his wife Michal.

David was worshipping the Lord at the head of a victorious parade as the Ark of the Covenant continued its journey to Jerusalem. It had been a long time in coming, having been in the hands of the Philistines for seven months. It was a historic moment, bursting with unfettered praise to God. As he danced, David wore only a linen ephod, a basic covering that exposed his bare arms and legs for easy movement. But it was less than the modest garment the customs of the Hebrew people required. No one noticed that day—except for Michal, his wife, the daughter of Saul, the previous king of Israel. She knew exactly how to act like royalty, and the little shepherd boy who was now king had a lot to learn about acting like a king. When he returned home, expecting a loving welcome from his wife, she mocked him for his actions and his dress.

It can be a bit of a shock to be on the receiving end of deceitful and dishonest behavior from someone you're dating. You're supposed to be putting your best foot forward (as Grandma used to say), building a future on hope and facts, only to realize your special someone isn't acting honorably.

Your first instinct may be to overlook or forgive the behavior or believe the denials and explanations that come later once they're exposed.

When you really like or love someone, you don't want to believe that they are capable of toxic behavior. You may not want to see it, because what would that say about you and your own judgment? "I'm drawn to toxic people." No one wants to think that.

Resist the temptation to make excuses for this person. The marriage relationship is too important to take chances. It's okay to detach kindly, firmly, and completely.

David likely didn't have much say in the choice of his spouse, but you do. You can walk away from a person who shows signs of being abusive, unfaithful, or disrespectful in any way.

LET'S PRAY

Lord, I want to serve You with all my heart. I want to find a partner who wants to do the same. Please give me the courage to walk away from anyone who turns out to not be right and also the wisdom to do it with grace and the strength to stand firm if they feel disappointed. Amen.

DAY 29

When the Good Is in the Way of the Best

Do two walk together unless they have agreed to do so?
AMOS 3:3

When Abram's brother, Haran, had died way back before their first trip out of their hometown, he had taken his nephew, Lot, under his wing, shared his wisdom, and given him direction. And Lot had blossomed into a successful man and leader. Abram could not have been prouder.

But now they were in a new land. Abram still loved Lot, and Lot continued to respect and love his uncle. Except their employees couldn't get along. Both men had grown so successful that their herders were quarreling. The land couldn't support both men's flocks. This couldn't go on. But the family ties were so great that they didn't want to separate, either.

So Abram the elder, against custom and protocol, offered Lot the first chance to choose the lands he would settle in. Lot saw the well-watered plains along the Jordan River and didn't have to think twice. Abram accepted the opposite direction. The men parted, rarely crossing paths in the coming years.

Saying goodbye to good people is especially difficult.

So it is with dating. Sometimes it takes a while to realize you're in a relationship with a wonderful person, but they are the wrong person for you. This is especially true when they are a person of good character. They are kind, loving, and pleasant, but for some reason, you know that you don't want to spend the rest of your life with them. It's not you, and it's not them. There's just no "us" in your futures.

God gives us choice in making these decisions. He won't force you into a relationship that is not sustainable long term. Yet He won't give you an escape from a difficult conversation with a good person most of the time, either. If anything, He expects you to use His wisdom to make the weighty decision of choosing a partner.

When Abram had to separate from Lot, it wasn't because he wasn't getting along with Lot or had stopped loving him. No, it was because the direction he was going in was different from the direction Lot was going in. Both remained good men.

Honesty and authenticity are required for parting with a good person. No one wants you to marry them out of pity. This is your opportunity to have a difficult conversation—a skill that you will need all through your lifelong romantic relationships.

Break up with that good person with kindness and finality. God will back up your choice. No matter how much it hurts in the short term, it's still the best decision for both of you.

LET'S PUT IT INTO PRACTICE

Prepare yourself to say no to a good relationship that might not be the best for you. Write out several breakup statements that you might share with a good person, pretending you are a diplomat in a tense situation who must speak honestly but also kindly to the other party.

Who's in Your Neighborhood?

Whoever has ears, let them hear.
MATTHEW 11:15

Because it's scattered across the Gospels, because it's phrases tucked inside longer verses, and because of many other factors, we often fail to recognize one of the great shocks in the New Testament—the siblings of the Messiah did not believe He was the Messiah. After His public ministry had begun, to the point that some were already seeking to kill Him, John 7:5 tells us, "For even his own brothers did not believe in him."

Then Paul writes that the resurrected Christ individually visited specific people, and James was visited before the apostles (1 Corinthians 15:7). James didn't believe his half brother was the Messiah until after Christ was crucified and resurrected. He became an instant believer and ended up bravely pastoring the first-century church through persecution and writing the New Testament book of James.

Unbelievable, right? How could he miss something that was right in front of his eyes? The best possible answer—until we're able to ask him about it in heaven—is that he clung to misconceptions for roughly 31 years and refused to see anything that contradicted that mindset. He literally missed out on appreciating the only perfect person in history.

And now we talk about examining our own misconceptions. We all know we have blind spots, but we too often fail to acknowledge them. If they're not outright prejudices, then we tell ourselves that those blind spots mostly don't matter. They're just part of being human.

It's how we justify overlooking worthy partners because they don't quite match our expectations. We've known them forever, or they seem so timid, or, yes, they have a job and a house, but do I want to become an instant parent if we get married? James had to believe that a Messiah wasn't supposed to be like his older, illegitimate brother, Jesus the carpenter. There was no prophecy for that description! James was completely justified in his own mind.

Sometimes the details we put into our head about what a relationship is supposed to look like can distract us from the true substance of friendship that could create a fulfilling, loving partnership. We might be hanging out or attending church with someone who meets our requirements except . . . well, where's the cool social media engagement when we're together? Where's the surprise? The mystery? Where's the huge upside of that new perfect partner pulling you into a different subculture full of curiosities and excitement?

Part of the problem of an idealized partner is how it dulls us to our own preconceptions and blind spots. Perfectly good romantic prospects—at church, at work, in our friend group, in our outside activities—are casually flattened because we think our personal prophecies point us to something different. Maybe they do. But maybe, if you're caught in a desert or in a rut, it might be time to reassess your personal mindset and look with fresh eyes at the wonderful people you already know.

LET'S REFLECT

Who are the people you currently know and like but haven't considered dating? You may have good reasons, and it's possible that they are not right for you. But it may also be that you classified them prematurely, and today might be a good day to reassess.

Don't Kill the Messenger

If any of you lacks wisdom, you should ask God,
who gives generously to all without finding
fault, and it will be given to you.
JAMES 1:5

A landowner in the ancient Middle East planted a vineyard, built a wall around it for protection, dug a winepress to turn the grapes into wine, and built a watchtower for easy oversight. Then he rented it to some local farmers with a deal to split the profits. When it was time to reap the profits of their joint efforts, he sent three representatives to collect his share. The farmers seized these representatives, beating one, killing another, and stoning a third. The landowner sent more representatives to the farmers, but all were treated the same. Finally, he sent his son, thinking that he would be respected as his heir. But the farmers killed him as well.

Jesus then asked what the landowner would do to the farmers (Matthew 21:33–45). The people replied, "He will bring those wretches to a wretched end." The farmers deliberately ignored the fact that their future livelihood and well-being depended on having a good working relationship with the owner. They just didn't want to share the current profits, and that was that. They had stuff they wanted to buy, and they chose to keep the money due to the landlord.

Why would anyone think this way? Because the desire to enjoy short-term pleasure can overpower the discipline to plan for long-term fulfillment. The messages pointing to healthy relationships and away from harmful relationships are all around. The question is, will we pay attention or will we kill the messenger?

Red flags are the easiest type of message to perceive. We need to hear those warnings. But there are other messages we often receive that are just as important. They're just not as dramatic, because they're small reminders to focus on self-improvement. We see a profile with language that gives us pause but think, "They're so cute. What could be the harm in chatting?"

Our romantic partner displays a temper at someone or tells a lie, but we dismiss the behavior because "They don't behave that way with me." We haven't had a date in six months, but we ignore the friend who encourages us to be proactive about meeting people, saying, "You don't understand just how busy I am!"

The messengers come with messages we don't want to hear. But they are calling us to long-term fulfillment. If we ignore them for too long, it kills the part of us that even registers the need to change. We end up stagnating or getting hurt.

It's not enough to pray for wisdom (James 1:5). We also must recognize wisdom when it arrives via a messenger we may not expect or want to hear from. It may include truths we don't want to face. We just have to decide whether we're going to be the farmers who respond humbly to the messenger or the farmers who kill the messenger.

LET'S REFLECT

Are there parts of your dating journey that you have been unwilling to change? Thoughts, patterns, habits, and responses that lead away from healthy, loving relationships but feel good in the moment? Take time today to be radically honest with yourself about these, and take the first steps to change them.

$\mathcal{D}$AY 32

How Not to Get on Reality TV

*Do not let any unwholesome talk come out of your mouths,
but only what is helpful for building others up according
to their needs, that it may benefit those who listen.*
EPHESIANS 4:29

There are entire accounts on social media completely focused on the awful interactions, horrible dates, and negative experiences people have on dating apps. There are still other accounts focused on screenshots of dating conversations between partners. All of these are carefully curated to guarantee maximum entertainment value.

Magazines and websites chronicle gossip, speculation, and gory details of celebrity love lives. Throw in the hilarious memes that make the rounds, reality TV that focuses on offering love connections in just about every possible setting—in a house! On an island! In a prison! On a sinking yacht! In a spaceship going to Mars! It is not hard to see that the media is putting a lot of effort into conditioning us to see dating as entertainment rather than a serious quest for an important result.

Nearly all of these outlets reflect the attitude that everyone is disposable. Every date is just a way to provide content for your Twitter feed or group texts. The human emotions behind the story are met with pity, laughter, or scorn rather than empathy.

When dating, you may find yourself being questioned constantly about the latest "happenings" by friends or others who want to be amused and entertained. This is different from the mentor or friend who is concerned and wants to lend support and wisdom. It doesn't mean that it's wrong to share a funny story from a date, but you don't want to be the person whose primary value is horrible dating stories. Your personal life is not a spectacle for your friends to see as a weekly sport.

Young John Mark deserted the apostles Barnabas and Paul on their first missionary journey, creating no end of bad feelings in the older men. Yet when he was given a second chance at a missionary journey with Barnabas, he did not repeat his earlier youthful mistakes. When next we hear of him, Paul is writing that John Mark is worthy of respect. Later, we learn that he was the author of the Gospel of Mark.

While you don't want to take yourself too seriously, you also don't want to make light of your journey. The search for a spouse is something that will define your path for many years to come. You can laugh at yourself and your situation when everything goes wrong. But there's a way to do that as a mature adult, not as the punch line for everyone else's jokes.

No matter how society treats those searching for a mate through dating, there's no reason you can't proceed on your journey with dignity.

So the next time your friends get together to connect over dating horror stories or tag you on their social media "worst of the apps" post, it's okay to change the subject, untag yourself, or gently set a boundary to let them know your life is not reality TV.

LET'S PUT IT INTO PRACTICE

Spend some time with Psalm 31:19–20. You could memorize it, write it on a nice piece of stationery, record yourself saying it, or anything else that feels meaningful to you. "How abundant are the good things that you have stored up for those who fear you, that you bestow in the sight of all, on those who take refuge in you. In the shelter of your presence you hide them from all human intrigues; you keep them safe in your dwelling from accusing tongues."

DAY 33

Wanting a Social Media–Worthy Relationship

But the Lord said to Samuel, "Do not consider his appearance or his height, for I have rejected him. The Lord does not look at the things people look at. People look at the outward appearance, but the Lord looks at the heart."
1 SAMUEL 16:7

No. Left swipe. No. Left swipe. Stop.

This guy's new. He's cute but doesn't seem to know how to dress himself. Lives in the boonies. Has never traveled but hopes to someday. Loves animals. Here's a picture of him playing a musical instrument . . . by himself. So he's not part of a band. Here's one with his brothers. Eep. He must've gotten the short genes in his family. Works for his dad. (Never a good sign, no initiative.)

No. Left swipe. No. Left swipe. No. Left swipe. Stop.

This guy here. Well then! I like that beard. And he's tall. Look at him! Taller than anyone else in his pictures. And muscles. Those are no ordinary muscles. Hello, my tall, dark, and handsome drink of water. Wait a minute. Those are national leaders in a couple of his pictures! How does he know them? Says he loves family, owns a start-up, and is an introvert. Some call him shy. So the strong, silent type? Sign me up.

Screenshot. Screenshot. Screenshot. Right swipe. I hope they pick me! Am I good enough for them? Send screenshots to besties. Now to find them on social media . . .

Anyone who has used a dating app knows all about instantaneous evaluations, the merging of pictures and text as the person they're looking at makes their best possible presentation.

Except it's almost always a public, appearance-driven presentation where the deeper, most important characteristics don't always get a chance to shine. Imagine if King David and King Saul—both before they were kings—were on that dating app we were swiping through. God told Samuel that people look at the outward appearance, but God looks at the heart (1 Samuel 16:7).

Saul seemed to have had nearly every physical advantage a man could have yet had no connection with God. When it came time for him to lead, he froze (instead of fighting Goliath), lost his nerve (with the Amalekites), and fell apart emotionally when God held him accountable.

We lionize David today because he cultivated a connection with God that created a long and (mostly) righteous reign. Except most of his dating app characteristics might not have been that impressive.

These days, it's easy to think that how good you look together (or *could* look together) and whether people call you cute or a "power couple" are the most important indicators of future fulfillment in your relationship. Yet what brings fulfillment in a relationship is emotional connection and emotional maturity. It's the hard work of prioritizing God and your significant other that rarely appears on social media.

Don't be tricked by society's priorities. Swipe right on a relationship that is as good on the inside as it is on the outside.

LET'S PRAY

Lord, it's hard for me to see what's behind the glitz and the glamour when I meet someone. It's easy for me to get caught up in the fairy tale in my head. Please open my eyes to see beyond what looks good to me and to see what is real to You so that I might choose rightly. Amen.

$\mathcal{D}$AY 34

Let's Be a Power Couple!

As iron sharpens iron, so one person sharpens another.
PROVERBS 27:17

When you think of the day-to-day life you want to build with your future partner, what does it look like? I know. Sometimes it's too painful to project an unknown future, but it's essential if you want to merge and achieve together.

Too often we cling to vague ideas about what we'll bring to the relationship, thinking that if it gets serious, our intrinsic strengths will shine through and be perfect for the situation. I'll be the funny one. I'll be the planner. I'll be the breadwinner. I'll cook perfect meals for them. I'll make sure they always feel loved and supported. I'll make sure they pursue their dreams. They'll take care of me.

None of that is wrong. But that's not a life. That's a bunch of stray ideas and unfocused passions. That's too similar to Samson and Delilah, where great passion kept them together but didn't help them know each other any better.

A better example might be Priscilla and Aquila, the tent-making teachers in the Acts of the Apostles. For being relatively unknown, they sure made a big impact on the first-century church. Not only did they minister to the Apostle Paul and mentor the gifted speaker Apollos when it came to the gospel, but they helped build the fledgling church in Ephesus in Asia Minor with Paul. Both were teachers, but the designation of Priscilla before Aquila indicates to scholars that she was likely the better teacher and may have been from a superior social stratum before marrying him. Some even speculate that she wrote the book of Hebrews. Together, they made a real impact because of their desire to combine their efforts into a common vision.

Dating is fun, and it should be. It's a series of adventures to new places and new experiences with someone who is excited to share them with you. However, when you are dating someone, you are also creating this new entity that is the relationship. It's a good idea to know what you want to build ahead of time. Even if you haven't met your partner yet, it can't hurt to start thinking through a relationship vision. Doing this early will guide you to choose someone compatible and who shares similar values with you.

What do you envision day-to-day life with your partner will look like? What activities will you participate in? Where will you go to church? How will you spend your free time together?

A relationship vision can be built around a strong sense of purpose, core values, and having a clear vision of what God has called you two to do, as well as God's guidance for future decisions so that you can continue to choose rightly. The clearer you are about this, the more likely you are to find your counterpart along the same spiritual path that you are traveling.

It's not a fool's errand but a believer's guide.

LET'S PUT IT INTO PRACTICE

Pray and then write in your journal about a vision for you and your future significant other. Assuming honesty and a love for God, what will your relationship core values be? What could be your common purpose? What parts of your purpose might remain separate?

A Journey of a Thousand Miles Includes Hurts and Bruises No One Wants

*Heal me, Lord, and I will be healed; save me and
I will be saved, for you are the one I praise.*
JEREMIAH 17:14

You know the problem with seeing dating as an adventure? Adventures reveal challenges that create scuffs, scabs, and bruises. Adventure heroes never make it out of any of their exploits without scars for their efforts, though they also usually end up with the big prize at the end.

Dating as an adult makes you vulnerable to a host of painful experiences. The rejection of strangers can feel deeply personal and painful. This rejection can create the worst thoughts from the deepest part of that dark night of the soul. When that happens, you will wonder where God is during this process. And He will be right there with you offering healing for your pain.

David's journey to become the king of Israel and secure the kingdom from its enemies took him through battle after battle. Sometimes they were psychological, sometimes they were spiritual, and sometimes they were physical. In the book of Psalms, he journaled his continual prayer to God for healing and sustenance: "Lord my God, I called to You for help, and You healed me" (Psalm 30:2).

If you're going after a worthwhile prize, then you must accept that hurtful setbacks will happen. Yes, they will sting. But you can take care of yourself when something goes sideways on your dating journey. That's what maturity is all about. Still, it's important to reach out for healing instead of sweeping the incidents under the rug. Bring every disappointment and betrayal to God so that the hurts don't take you out of the adventure.

Start by honestly identifying how you feel about the situation. Don't downplay its effects. You may be tempted to put on a brave face for others, but you can let your guard down and show your true feelings to God. Pour your heart out without censoring yourself, and He will be there for you.

Next, let Scripture speak to you. Do a search for words on God's "love" or "healing" or "wisdom." There is little that comforts so well as God's Word. Then ask, "What do I need to learn through this?" Embracing the lessons of the pain will protect you from it being repeated in the future.

Finally, open up to a friend, family member, mentor, or counselor. How much you share is up to you. But just letting someone know you're going through a hard moment can bring you healing, because you have a connection with someone who cares about you.

God wants to be there with you every step of the way. Let Him heal you by being open to His presence, His Word, and His people.

LET'S PRAY

Father, here I am—facing another hurt. Please give me perspective as I journey into areas where my heart is vulnerable, my emotions raw, and my mind aflame with fears. Help me learn how to heal quickly so that I might be a testimony of Your grace. Amen.

But I've Tried Everything!

Then he said, "Take the arrows," and the king took them.
Elisha told him, "Strike the ground." He struck it three
times and stopped. The man of God was angry with him
and said, "You should have struck the ground five or six
times; then you would have defeated Aram and completely
destroyed it. But now you will defeat it only three times."
2 KINGS 13:18–19

No matter what goal we've set for ourselves, there will be mental obstacles that stand in the way of us being successful. One of the most common is the frustrating feeling that we've done everything possible to achieve the goal and been completely unsuccessful and there's nothing more we can do.

A woman once declared in despair, "I've done all I can! I've been looking for a partner for over seven years!" However, further investigation into the details of her efforts revealed that she had dated just four people during the seven years. That wasn't what you would expect when she said "everything."

Elisha could relate. He was old and near death. Israel was being raided by the Moabites and battling Aram (Syria). King Jehoash came to the legendary man of God, acolyte of the fire-breathing Elijah, crying at his impending death. Elisha ignored the weeping and told the king to get a bow and arrows. Once they arrived, an arrow was notched in the bowstring, Elisha put his hands on the king's, and they shot the arrow out the window of the house. Elisha declared this the Lord's arrow of victory over Aram at Aphek.

Then he gave the king an unusual order. Gather the remaining arrows in his hand and strike the ground. The king, probably feeling uncomfortable and a bit confused, struck the ground three times with the arrows.

The prophet became angry, telling the king he should have struck the ground five or six times and that would have guaranteed Aram would be completely destroyed. Instead, he would only defeat them in battle three times. In his mind, King Jehoash had done everything he could, but he underestimated the challenge at hand and the effort it would require.

We also underestimate what it might take to find our person and declare that we've done everything but nothing's working. While it might be true that you haven't succeeded yet and the journey might even be harder for you than others, ask yourself whether this is where you want your love story to end.

Waving the white flag and saying you've tried everything might feel good for a minute, because it gives you a way out. It gives you permission to give up.

But radical honesty calls you to ask yourself whether you really did everything.

Is it possible you can do more? Are there parts of your comfort zone that you haven't left yet? Could you strike the arrow a few more times on the way to win the prize?

And when you win the prize, that's when you'll know you did everything you could.

LET'S PRAY

Lord, help me not cheat myself of a loving relationship by giving less of myself than I am capable of. Help me understand that You put more within me than I realize and that with Your grace I can run this race so that victory will be mine. Amen.

DAY 37

Turn Fears into Requests

Do not be anxious about anything, but in
every situation, by prayer and petition, with
thanksgiving, present your requests to God.
PHILIPPIANS 4:6

Remember the parable of the talents? A man gives three servants his money before he leaves on a long trip. Two servants double their money through hard work. The other servant hides his money away from fear until the master returns, at which point he is condemned while the other two are welcomed into the master's presence. Here is a dating retelling:

A famous matchmaker called three single friends together to help them find their perfect person. The first friend was given a new wardrobe, unlimited use of a beachfront condo, and a Lamborghini.

The next friend was given two gifts: friendship with the most popular musician in the world and unlimited use of a yacht.

The final friend was given the world's greatest comic book collection, which she could share on social media but not sell. So while the first two friends told the world about their good fortune and doubled their number of dates, the third friend decided the less anyone knew about this comic book collection the better. She put it all in the basement and carried on as if she didn't have it.

Sometimes it can feel like there's no one out there who would be the right match for your particular personality and quirks.

You might be an introvert who needs a lot of alone time to feel at ease, and you worry that your future partner might feel neglected or not understand your need to be alone. You worry that stepping into the dating pool, with all of the associated conversations, dates in public places, and other interactions, will force you to change into an extrovert in order to cultivate a relationship.

You might come from a family that is super close—going on large family vacations together—and you worry that your future partner might not enjoy being with your loud, rambunctious family members.

You might have big dreams to live in Africa or have seven children, and you worry that there just isn't anyone out there who would want the same thing, so why bother? After all, you've already been teased about it by your friends and family, and it would be humiliating to be rejected by a romantic interest over it.

Editing out parts of yourself that you think will be unacceptable in the dating world is the wrong move. Don't be alarmed by your quirks and uniqueness. The psalmist says you are fearfully and wonderfully made (Psalm 139:14). That means you are a unique person overladen with talents and challenges.

And so is everyone else. The person who will be an appropriate partner for you will have unique traits that make them a fit for you. You also will have unique traits and the best personality to make you a fit for them. This is not a problem. This is how it's supposed to work.

So instead of using your uniqueness as an obstacle or reason why a relationship just isn't possible for you, remember that God is on your side on the journey. He gave you your unique traits for a reason, and they are the perfect complement for your person.

LET'S PUT IT INTO PRACTICE

List the things you think are obstacles to you finding a partner ("I am an introvert, and no one will understand my need for alone time"). Rewrite your list with each problem phrased as a prayer: "Lord, help me find a partner who would understand and celebrate my need for alone time."

I'll Love You Just the Way I Change You

This matter arose because some false believers had infiltrated our ranks to spy on the freedom we have in Christ Jesus and to make us slaves. We did not give in to them for a moment, so that the truth of the gospel might be preserved for you.
GALATIANS 2:4-5

When we meet someone we like, it's tempting to want to project our wants and desires on them and try to change them instead of accepting them for who they are.

We like to romanticize the early church in the book of Acts. We think of them as perfect, loving, and kind. In truth, they were just humans, filled with the Holy Spirit, trying to figure out how to live victorious Christian lives with each other and among nonbelievers.

They still suffered from pride, envy, and poor communication. And when non-Jewish people began joining the church, the Jewish Christians suffered spiritual shock. They couldn't imagine sharing their new community with the uncircumcised, pork-eating Gentile Christians who didn't keep the Sabbath.

There was a group of Jewish Christians, well meaning but dogmatic, who insisted that the Gentile Christians of Antioch must get circumcised (Acts 15). Men getting circumcised was a requirement to be Jewish, a tradition that dated to the days of Abraham. They opened their arms to the Gentiles, but only under the condition that they change and conform to Jewish ideas and traditions.

When we meet someone we like, we want them to be everything we want so that we can be at the end of our journey. If we hold on to this desire for them to fit our picture, we will stray into control. Control means that we want the world and the people in it to be the way we want so we can avoid disappointment and be assured that we will have what we want.

Anytime that special person does something outside our prescribed desire, it creates disappointment, which shows up in different ways: withdrawal, anger, petulance, anxiety, people pleasing, and even sadness. And then we blame them for how we feel. It's a human response. But it's not wise.

As in the case of the well-meaning Jewish Christians in Acts, it's often difficult to recognize the urge to control others within us, because it often comes from a good place. "This will help them," we tell ourselves. "If they improve themselves in this one area, they'll be better and happier."

All of it might be true. Yet if we apply pressure, no matter how subtle, to control their actions, then we're the ones in the wrong. Control is not an attribute of love. Love calls us to respect the autonomy of the other person.

Peace in life comes from knowing the difference between what we can control and what we cannot control. People are not ours to control, and for sure your future partner will not be someone you can control. Nor should you want to.

LET'S PUT IT INTO PRACTICE

The Serenity Prayer written by Reinhold Niebuhr has been memorized and prayed by millions of people on the path of releasing control and practicing acceptance. Look up and memorize the full Serenity Prayer, and say it when you are tempted to change, fix, or otherwise improve others to suit yourself.

DAY 39

Looking Back for the One Who Got Away

Forgetting what is behind and straining toward what is ahead, I press on toward the goal to win the prize for which God has called me heavenward in Christ Jesus.
PHILIPPIANS 3:13–14

It's only natural to romanticize past relationships, especially if we haven't found another one we are happy with. As time passes, the pain fades, and we forget the cracks in the relationship that caused it to end. The old days begin to look more and more attractive, and we find ourselves playing the game of "What If?"

"What if they were 'the One'?"

"What if I'd been wiser and not so clueless?"

"What if I hadn't broken up with them?"

After Israel's first king, Saul, failed to listen to the Lord's instructions via Samuel to destroy the evil Amalekites, God disowned Saul. However, Samuel, the prophet who had anointed Saul, had a soft spot for him.

Samuel did his best to rectify the Amalekite situation. Long after God had moved on, Samuel continued to mourn Saul's failures as king. In spite of knowing that Saul had failed the nation of Israel, Samuel had trouble letting him go. Samuel was mourning the past king while God had a better king waiting. He mourned so long that God finally had to elbow Samuel out of his depression and make him move on and go anoint the new king of Israel.

Sometimes, in the quiet moments or in the middle of the night, we silently curse ourselves for the mistakes we've made, the opportunities we remained blind to, the wrong one we stayed too long with, or that special someone who slipped through our fingers.

Maybe it was our fault or maybe it was their fault or maybe the job or family got in the way, but all we know now is we're lonely and the current dating opportunities look mighty weak and . . . well, they might've been "the One." It's the devil you know, even if it was destroying you.

The regrets are understandable, but the worst part of this process is not the loss but the trap of always looking backward. It is often easier to look back at what is familiar rather than work on something we cannot see. You can't find your future if you're looking back into the past. You can't fulfill God's will today if you're mourning Saul. You can't appreciate the opportunities God puts right in front of you when you are focused on replaying images of the past.

Lot's wife is the Bible's poster child for looking back. The angels insisted Lot and all his family leave Sodom before its imminent destruction. Lot, his wife, and their two single daughters all raced from Sodom and Gomorrah after being given clear instructions: *Don't look back*. As the city blazed in destruction, Lot's wife looked back. God turned her into a pillar of salt.

Looking back freezes you in the past and drains you of the energy, attention, and focus you need to create the future. Choose the future, because God already has your King David waiting for you.

LET'S REFLECT

Take an honest look at how often you might be indulging in rehashing past relationships as a way to escape engaging with challenges in the present. Resolve to redirect your thoughts back to the present with hope and belief that you can create the future you want.

Loving Those Who Hate You

You love those who hate you and hate those who love you.
2 SAMUEL 19:6

General Joab was furious with King David. And King David deserved the fury. The nation of Israel had just suffered through its second civil war and barely came out intact. The king's favorite son, Absalom, had split the nation; created his own army; taken the capital, Jerusalem, once David abandoned it; proclaimed his kingship atop the palace; and then gathered his forces for a brutal attack on David's men.

Despite this rebellion, David had instructed his generals to treat Absalom gently in battle. General Joab would have none of it. When given the chance, he killed Absalom, knowing he would only continue to sow insurrection within the nation if he were allowed to live. Absalom's forces immediately scattered.

When the news of this victory arrived, David asked persistently about the fate of his son and then broke down weeping when he heard of his death. Soon, the victorious army was slinking into the city beneath the wailing. Joab realized that David was about to turn victory into defeat and reprimanded the king for caring more for Absalom than for the brave men who had defended him. This woke David up, and he appeared in public, confirming the victory.

There's a lot of truth in the "love those who hate you and hate those who love you" (2 Samuel 19:6) phrase when it comes to dating.

We think that because we are a steady Christian, someone like us would be too boring, and we need the bad boy or the edgy gal to balance us out. We don't want to appear too predictable.

We want to capture the attention of the worship leader, preacher, or person voted "most likely to succeed" in the youth group and turn down the smart, funny friend because we've "known them forever."

When dating, we can get addicted to the euphoria of extreme highs of romance and excitement. Sometimes the relationships that create the highest highs feel that way not because of real love but because of drama.

The intense infatuation that blocks out any sense of responsibility. Jealousy.

Exclusivity that isolates you from friends and family.

The constant conflict that brings the depths of despair and the incredible relief of making up and being together again.

Healthy love is exciting, but it is also simultaneously peaceful and calm. It doesn't create a division between your person and other things or people in your life that you value. Rather, it protects and nurtures everything you value.

David valued his love for Absalom over the safety and security of the kingdom. Without the wisdom of Joab, David would have sacrificed it all for his spoiled, backstabbing son.

There is a type of relationship that will ask you to sacrifice your peace of mind, safety, and security to be "in love." This type of relationship is toxic and unhealthy. Be ready to recognize it and avoid it. Because the high today is not worth the crash at the end.

LET'S PRAY

Lord, help me develop the self-awareness and discernment required so that I can tell the difference between infatuation and real love. Give me the wisdom to practice romantic love in a way that is calm and peaceful and upholds my core values. Amen.

Boundaries Are the New Black

Whoever walks in integrity walks securely, but
whoever takes crooked paths will be found out.
PROVERBS 10:9

In the days before cannons and rifles, a city's reputation centered almost entirely around the strength of its walls. It was often that and not the strength of an army that determined its survival.

There was no city mightier than Constantinople, which had three walls surrounding the city, each inner wall taller than the previous wall to defend the city. Ancient Jericho's walls were so thick that they could drive chariots across the top of them and people lived within them.

There was only one city that defied this walled wisdom, and that was ancient Sparta (650 BC), which had no walls. The warriors of Sparta were so legendarily savage that they defied enemies to attack—and lived.

Just as every city has its walls, so we must decide what type of boundaries we must erect as we pursue love. When you fall in love, you get swept up in a flow of heightened emotions. This is totally normal, but it can also cause you to make questionable decisions. As you spend more and more time with a person you are drawn toward, it's easy to forget who you are as you move toward becoming a beautiful "we." There is a healthy way to be a part of a couple and an unhealthy way.

It's important when dating to maintain your individual connection with God, your purpose, and your personality while continuing to make your own adult decisions and fulfill the responsibilities in your life. The couple becomes stronger when the individuals are clear about their own strengths and weaknesses.

Like city walls, boundaries help you maintain your sense of self, personal security, and self-confidence. Without them, you begin to look to others for validation and approval. You lose touch with what you want out of life and how to ask for it with confidence.

At some point, you will have rapturous feelings for a partner. The euphoria of being in love can easily make an idol out of the relationship. Instead of pleasing God, pleasing your partner becomes your top priority. Healthy boundaries are the walls that keep you in integrity on your personal walk with God. It's not a matter of if but when you will need to set boundaries to keep you and your relationship on the right track.

When you have healthy boundaries, you know who you are, you remember and participate in your hobbies, you spend time alone and with your old friends and your family. And your partner should do the same. It's healthy for there to be a clear "you," "me," and "we."

LET'S REFLECT

As you date, reflect on whether you are able to maintain your personal values, friendships, and interests while with the other person. Are they threatened by the life you have apart from them? Is your personal growth flourishing or slowing down? Which boundaries can you set to benefit yourself and your relationship?

Difficult Conversations

*Wounds from a friend can be trusted, but
an enemy multiplies kisses.*
PROVERBS 27:6

Peter was the apostle who preached on the day of Pentecost, and he was the one who brought the gospel to the Gentiles. Yet when he visited the Gentile revival church in Antioch (modern-day Turkey), some Jewish Christians arrived from Jerusalem and snubbed the Gentile Christians and refused to eat with them. Peter caved in to the peer pressure and joined the Jewish clique.

So Paul, also a Jew, decided to have a difficult conversation with Peter. He stood up and called Peter out in front of the entire congregation for trying to pressure Gentiles to act like Jews when in reality they were all Christians and Christ had removed the separation between Jews and Gentiles. Paul's willingness to hold Peter accountable prevented a split in the early church.

In healthy relationships, it's important that both individuals have the skill and maturity to discuss difficult topics openly and honestly. You and your partner will come together with different personalities, boundaries, and likes and dislikes and other areas of mismatch (hopefully few!). You each also have faults and mistakes and errors in judgment (hopefully not major!).

Growing a healthy relationship requires the art of having a difficult conversation. Difficult conversations are less about conflict resolution and more about authentic expression and accountability around important situations: money, sex, parenting, chores, birth family interactions, and even where to spend the holidays.

The point of knowing who you are is that you share the real you with your partner. And this means not just the fun things. How do you both manage money? It's important to discuss this with your partner and ask them what seem like awkward questions about their own financial status. Do either of you have preferences or situations that might require an adjustment from a long-term partner? A health condition, a family situation, plans to live in your current town forever? Definitely disclose these to a new partner.

But disclosure is only half of a difficult conversation. Asking questions that require your partner's disclosure is the other half. Verbalizing discomfort at something your partner does or doesn't do is also required.

Sharing openly and requesting open conversation with a future partner help you know truly whether you are both suited for each other or whether there are incompatibilities that could make a healthy relationship difficult or even impossible. When everything is out in the open, you can negotiate, recreate, or decide to walk away.

Unfortunately, many couples do not practice the art of the difficult conversation until after the wedding, and then they are surprised at their partner's response to their boundaries and preferences. Some couples avoid these conversations and sweep important issues under the rug, eventually drifting apart from each other.

If you grew up in a family that practiced open and honest communication, you might be lucky enough to have had it modeled for you. If not, this is a skill you need to learn and practice while dating and throughout marriage.

LET'S PUT IT INTO PRACTICE

Make a list of topics that you would need to explore and discuss with a significant other at an appropriate time in the relationship. Keep the list where you can easily retrieve it when you need it. Add topics to the list whenever something comes to mind.

Day 43

Working Through
Inevitable Conflict

*Do not make friends with a hot-tempered person, do
not associate with one easily angered, or you may
learn their ways and get yourself ensnared.*
PROVERBS 22:24–25

Everyone wants the same dating journey: fall in love with our
one true love on the first date. "We both love Korean food, so
we ended up sharing food, and we kept talking until we closed
the restaurant down. Then we talked in the parking lot for an hour,
and I realized she was something special."

Or the love at first sight version: "I turned the corner and bumped
right into him! As we were picking up my things off the floor, he looked
into my eyes, and I just knew he was the one."

The reality is that most of those dating myths and movies don't
include the real-life emotional challenges that come with a relationship. Even with a magical beginning, conflicts will arise along
the way. What makes this difficult is that you can't always prepare
for what type of conflict you might face. Conflict is not always
muted disagreements between two calm adults. There will likely be
full-blown arguments, long angry silences, and words that you might
later wish you hadn't shared.

Conflict will come up for different reasons. You might be with a
person who is a good match for you but be working out the kinks
in the relationship. You might be with a person who is not a good
fit for you and for whom you are not a good fit, and the constant
arguments and pain keep coming up to show you that you are not

a match. Your counterpart might be a truly angry, contentious, or even abusive person whom you should not be dating at all.

When you're mired in any of those situations (or others that are similar), what you must keep in the forefront of your mind is that there is inappropriate anger and appropriate anger. It is the difference between the violent, destructive anger of Cain and the corrective, boundary-setting anger of Christ.

Cain's anger came from a proud streak in his character. He resented Abel for offering an acceptable sacrifice. He refused to look at the fact that he had disobeyed the Lord. He allowed that anger to simmer until it boiled over and he killed his brother. Then he got surly with God afterward. He embodied his anger. It was not a tool; it was his mindset.

Christ's anger was righteous. It was focused on the actions of the money-grubbers who were corrupting the house of God. His anger was directed at people who hurt the vulnerable.

The Apostle Paul wrote, "In your anger do not sin" (Ephesians 4:26). Conflict in your relationship is inevitable, but how you choose to fight and resolve conflict is up to you. The choice of a partner who gets angry but is not an angry or abusive person is also up to you.

LET'S REFLECT

Think about your current conflict resolution skills. Do you avoid conflict? Escalate it? Passively stand by? What about your partner's conflict resolution skills? How do they respond when conflict comes up? Are your skills at a level to sustain a successful long-term relationship? Make a plan to improve your skills—alone or with your partner.

DAY 44

Looking for Love in All the Wrong Places

*Though my father and mother forsake
me, the Lord will receive me.*
PSALM 27:10

Is your first act of the morning to grab your phone and check for a text from the person you matched with on the app a few days ago? If they've reached out, your heart soars, but if they haven't, your heart sinks, and you begin to ruminate on what might be wrong. This can be normal when dating, but if you find your emotions constantly swinging from high to low based on what a romantic interest does or doesn't do, there may be a deeper issue.

Sometimes the search for a romantic partner masks a deeper fear of abandonment. Without fully recognizing it, we do not feel whole within ourselves, and we hope that being with someone will heal the loneliness and help us finally feel complete and right in the world. We fantasize, romanticize, and obsess over romantic partners as a way to escape inner dissatisfaction.

Fearing abandonment makes you hold on to people who are not healthy for you, because the feeling of being alone is unbearable. This tendency might show itself while dating but also among your primary friend group or even settling for wonderful coworkers while everyone knows you're working together for a toxic company that treats you like a number.

There are several signs that you might be struggling with a fear of abandonment. Most people experience these things from time to time in their lives, but if these patterns are repeating for you, it's worth noticing.

- You feel like you don't belong anywhere—whether you are at work, with family, or even with most of your friend group while wondering why these aren't "my people."

- You are sensitive to rejection and feel that people constantly reject you.

- You are no longer a teenager, yet you still choose partners you know aren't a strong long-term match to avoid being alone.

- You attach too quickly to that special someone who may not actually be that special. But then breakups are messy.

- You often compromise your personal standards as a way to hold on to relationships.

- You feel starved of love.

Healing the pain of abandonment will create a foundation of emotional security. Being emotionally secure means you no longer use others' actions to regulate your emotions. You can feel calm, worthy, and lovable no matter the situation.

If you've experienced a difficult childhood, traumatic breakup, or the loss of a parent, you may need therapy, counseling, or coaching to deal with the feelings of abandonment. If you do not get help for this soul wound, you will likely project this emotional dishevelment onto the people you date; it can also cloud your judgment when choosing a partner. Take a fearless self-evaluation of your actions and act upon it.

LET'S PUT IT INTO PRACTICE

As you date this week, check in frequently with your moods and emotions. How do you feel before and after a date? How do you feel when texting and communicating with romantic partners? Keep a log for a week to see whether you have a healthy calm or you are experiencing an emotional roller coaster. Ask for help if you need it.

$\mathcal{D}$AY 45

God's Love and Your Lovability

God has said, "Never will I leave you;
never will I forsake you."
HEBREWS 13:5

Rejection and indifference sometimes appear to be our default experience: a grumpy boss who never notices your accomplishments; coworkers who are more interested in themselves than in hearing about your life; family members and friends who seem too busy with their own lives to connect to yours; fellow believers at church who say you're part of the church family yet rarely try to contact you away from the church; swipe rights who rarely swipe right in return; the dates, the coffees, the Zoom calls that go nowhere. There's no frisson.

Sure, you might have that exemplary job or outstanding ministry or charity that is changing the world, but are you loved for who you are? Are you prized for who you are inside and out, no matter whether your life is going great or plummeting? And if you're not overtly loved as that person, does that mean you're unlovable?

Too often, too many of us chase a romantic relationship because we think it will prove that we are lovable and/or worthy of love. After all, a hollow social calendar grabs no one's attention, but laughing pictures on social media with a special someone in an interesting setting, a guaranteed significant other at events with acquaintances—not just family or great friends—inviting you to attend events because of your obvious coupledom, and even getting that extra attention from the other believers at church after service . . . that proves you're lovable, doesn't it?

Does it? People often wait until they are in a romantic relationship before they feel that they are lovable or worthy of love. But it's not true. You are worthy of love whether or not you happen to have found the person who chooses to love you in that specific way.

Just because Hollywood is incapable of making movies about healthy single people who can fill their lives with goodness and satisfaction while still seeking their perfect partner doesn't mean you can't live that life. Frankly, no partner can fulfill you or complete you, despite what the movies and songs want us to think. No partner can fill your love tank, but when you stay actively connected to the truth about how much God loves you, you can walk around with your love tank full all the time.

Yes, God can't wrap His arms around you in front of a cozy fireplace, but He can fill your heart and your life with peace and contentment. God is the true standard of whether we are lovable, and here's what He says specifically about you:

"The Lord appeared to us in the past, saying: 'I have loved you with an everlasting love; I have drawn you with unfailing kindness.'" (Jeremiah 31:3)

"Can a mother forget the baby at her breast and have no compassion on the child she has borne? Though she may forget, I will not forget you!" (Isaiah 49:15)

These verses become real when we live an active faith.

LET'S REFLECT

Feeling like you can't have or express love unless you have also found romantic love is a cultural lie. Reflect on God's love, things in your life you love, and those who currently love you. Doing this will activate love inside you that is not dependent on the outside world.

$\mathcal{D}$AY 46

Time to Take Center Stage

*Search me, God, and know my heart; test
me and know my anxious thoughts.*
PSALM 139:23

G ideon was hiding as Midianite raiders seemed to be every-where. An angel appeared before him and proclaimed, "The Lord is with you, mighty warrior." Gideon replied, "Pardon me, my lord, but if the Lord is with us, why has all this happened to us?" The angel said, "Go in the strength you have and save Israel out of Midian's hand. Am I not sending you?" (Judges 6:12–14).

And so, even though it was unconventional, Gideon did just that. He saved Israel through God's grace. He defeated the Midianites in battle, he created a 40-year peace, and he humbly refused to accept the people's demand that he become king, instead choosing to remain their judge. He made mistakes, but he accomplished his mission. It turns out he had it in him all along to be a leader; he just didn't know himself. Denial about who we are keeps us in our comfort zone.

There's a reason denial is such an easy option to pursue—self-discovery can be scary. A true personal inventory can be uncomfortable. We are often afraid that we will not like what we find when we turn the spotlight on ourselves. We might be afraid that all of our insecurities and things we dislike about ourselves are actually true. Who wants to be transparent when we can pretend those weaknesses aren't there?

Yet self-discovery actually helps you fully integrate all the parts of yourself into one whole person. Accepting yourself fully—the good, the bad, the ugly, the wonderful—gives you a springboard from which you can express yourself authentically throughout the dating journey, because you understand yourself. Unless you fully accept yourself, you may find yourself shrinking and changing to try to find a partner. After all, compromising that part of yourself when everything else seems to fit isn't that big of a deal, is it? It's working for everyone else.

You can despair that you may not find anyone who matches your own uniqueness. (You know who you are.) Yet Scripture points to the opposite supposition. The only prophet and judge in the Bible was a woman named Deborah whose responsibilities also transformed her into a warrior. She was married to a man comfortable with her higher standing, who appreciated her unique calling and talents.

Remember: We all have the responsibility to live up to our highest potential, and grappling with our weaknesses can help us express our deepest truths. It is in knowing yourself that you can live consciously without losing yourself and be authentic with a new partner. Knowing yourself is critical for making a match that lasts. And since that's our goal, working hard to achieve it becomes easier even when we're looking into the complex fun house mirror of our own soul.

LET'S PRAY

Lord, I recognize that sometimes I want to shrink back and edit myself down so that I can fit in with the people I meet. It's hard to stand out from others or to feel like my principles and standards scare potential partners away. Help me stay true to who You have called me to be in every way. Amen.

DAY 47

Relationship Principles over Relationship Rules

I have seen something else under the sun: The race is not to the swift or the battle to the strong, nor does food come to the wise or wealth to the brilliant or favor to the learned; but time and chance happen to them all.
ECCLESIASTES 9:11

Jesus and His disciples were walking through a grain field on the Sabbath when those crazy disciples of His started picking some grain to eat. I mean, you know why—James was always hungry day and night, while Andrew, Thomas, and Bartholomew had missed breakfast (night people are like that, aren't they?), and Thomas was always chewing on some long-stemmed something or other since before he started following Jesus.

The Pharisees, who always hovered on the edges of Jesus's ministry like a cloud of troublesome gnats, gasped in horror, "We helped Moses make rules about situations like this! You can't pluck food on the Sabbath! You're a bad Hebrew!" Jesus shook His head and then reminded these pearl-clutching busybodies that David—the man after God's own heart—entered the house of God and ate consecrated bread, which is lawful only for priests to eat. Plus, he gave some to his hungry men. Then Jesus declared, "The Sabbath was made for man, not man for the Sabbath" (Mark 2:23–27). Or, in today's language, Jesus might have said, "Stop it with all these rules! The Sabbath isn't what's important here. It's the people God made who are important."

Sometimes when we're dating, we get caught up in everybody else's rules:

- You must date for X months before you can get serious.

- The man should always make more money than the woman.

- Both partners must attend the same church.

- If they're still alive, your parents must approve of this person you're dating.

- Don't post your dates together on social media.

Yet somehow, in every society in the world over thousands of years, people have figured out how to find partners without these rules. Yes, you should have a personal code that has your own unmovable priorities within it, but most of what will make you part of the perfect partnership will be built around the flexibility of principles. Principles find the freedom within the rules that matter. Principles like setting boundaries, spending time with God daily, making peace with your past, forgiving often, setting goals, maintaining a growth mindset, and pursuing mutual reciprocity will create a merging of individuals into a reborn whole.

Being reborn together means creating a path uniquely your own in surrender to a loving God. It means others will not understand every choice you make and may even be angry or offended despite the peace of God you both feel about it. Remember that God loves us and wants to provide for us even as we seek communion together with Him.

LET'S PUT IT INTO PRACTICE

Make a list of things you learned how to do in the past few years (or decades). What did you think about those things before you learned about them, and what do you understand about them now? Compare how you think about dating with what you used to think about those things.

One Soul Mate or Many?

Do not be yoked together with unbelievers. For what
do righteousness and wickedness have in common?
Or what fellowship can light have with darkness?
2 CORINTHIANS 6:14

It was unthinkable just a few years back: Purchase three or four streaming channels, and you'll remain in entertainment heaven for the rest of your life. Movies, sports, TV series, comedy specials, and more are all waiting for you as soon as you click on your television. The choices never stop.

But . . . what if we added a wrinkle? What if those very same streaming services returned to those bad old days of television when certain shows were only on at certain times and there was no way to record them? You either watched at the weekly show time or you missed the show entirely. Then, about 13 weeks later, you had to suffer through something called "reruns." How much would we be willing to pay for services like that?

And then what if your mother decided you could only watch one show a week? Soon, you would be planning your entire week around that one show, refusing to leave the house on your special night on the off chance you would get delayed or distracted and miss your show.

Often, we treat the search for the perfect partner as if we're children suffering through the bad old days of television. Too often we think there is only one soul mate in this vast world, and we must reorganize our life around simply one longshot option, because that is the will of God.

The reality is that dating is much closer to today's streaming services—there is an endless supply of choices. There are many choices who could be a good spouse that we could enjoy and grow old with. This is similar to the seven deacons who were appointed to look after the Greek widows of the early church (Acts 6:1–6). None of these deacons was perfect, but they were clearly superior to the others in their integrity and trustworthiness and up to the challenges of the moment.

The number of choices can create decision paralysis in which we keep thinking that there might be someone better out there, so we don't want to make a decision or commitment when one swipe right will reveal our dream come true. So the date ends, and instead of taking the time to evaluate how we feel about it and what the next step may or may not be, it's easier to binge through more choices on a dating app. Or multiple dating apps. (Biblically, this is akin to Solomon and his 700 wives and 300 concubines.)

"The will of God" is sometimes preached as this super narrow choice from which disaster will arise if you miss it. In reality, God's will is a lot more forgiving and a much wider space. There is no perfect choice God demands you make, but godly choices that will enhance your life and walk with Him. You must decide how you pursue this for His glory and your peace of mind.

LET'S REFLECT

God's will is not a pinched set of rules but rather a loving generosity in feeling comfortable in Him. Look at other areas of your life—work, friendships, living options—where God has provided choices. How does that make you feel? Can you view your choice of spouse in the same way?

The Echo of an Eternal Infatuation

Those who work their land will have abundant food,
but those who chase fantasies have no sense.
PROVERBS 12:11

Narcissus was the most attractive human hunter in the ancient Roman world. Women swooned in his presence. The trail of broken hearts he left behind was legendary. Every woman should've known better than to try to get his attention, as haughty and condescending as he could be, but maybe he had to settle down with someone, right? So they kept trying.

The lovely forest nymph Echo was one of those enamored with Narcissus. However, she had a special challenge. Jupiter's wife, Juno, had punished Echo because she talked too much. So Juno cursed Echo with the inability to speak on her own. All she could do was repeat the last words of others.

So Echo found herself unable to get the attention of Narcissus, who often found himself the most interesting person in the room anyway. Still, Echo wouldn't release her total infatuation with the handsome hunter and made every attempt to communicate with him. When Narcissus would hunt in the forest, Echo would stalk him from behind trees in hopes they might connect.

Ever found yourself planning your route in the hope that you will run into a crush? Or building an imaginary love story with the perfect specimen who liked your comment on their social media post?

One day, Echo and Narcissus did connect. Narcissus found himself separated from his hunting party and called out, "Is anyone there?" Echo replied, "Is anyone there?" A startled Narcissus said, "Come here." Echo rushed toward the startled Narcissus as she repeated the command. Narcissus did not return Echo's love, but still, she remained infatuated.

We all know what happened to the arrogant Narcissus—Nemesis, the goddess of revenge, cast a spell on him so that when he saw his reflection in water, he fell in love with himself. Eventually, he wasted away and died.

However, Echo couldn't release her obsession with the unobtainable Narcissus. As a result, she began wasting away, losing her youth and her looks, until all that remained was her voice. Surrounded by a world full of things to do and people to love, she gave up real life for her hyperfocus on Narcissus.

When you find yourself in an imaginary relationship with someone you are crushing on, it's important to pull yourself out of your head and back into the real world.

Staying grounded in the real world with genuine interactions with friends and fellow believers can help you release the fantasy relationship in your head or on social media. It means accepting a life without filters to live a real faith with real people.

The world in our head or on social media can be more fun. But a genuine counterpart means engaging in this slow, ordinary physical world so that we don't become a shadow of our real selves: the real selves God made exactly as He intended so that we could find the person He made exactly for us.

LET'S PUT IT INTO PRACTICE

Keep a journal close at hand today. Throughout the day, make a note of how often your mind becomes distracted and starts to build a story about other people inside your head. Raising your awareness about the habit will help you take control of your thoughts and return to living in the real world.

Walking the Love Walk

When I was a child, I talked like a child, I thought like a child, I reasoned like a child. When I became a man, I put the ways of childhood behind me.
1 CORINTHIANS 13:11

Two people meet. They both feel that unexpected connection. Late-night texts and phone calls. Holding hands. The first kiss. Walks at sunset. Fancy restaurants. Excited conversations with friends because "This could be 'the One.'" Becoming official on social media. Low-level disagreements followed by making up. Meet the family. The proposal.

The wedding. Reading 1 Corinthians 13 during the ceremony. Joyous reception. Someone gives the couple a framed copy of 1 Corinthians 13 to hang up. Couple heads off into the sunset. Movie ends.

But real life still goes on. We know that 1 Corinthians 13 is the epitome, the very definition, of a mature love. And living out the love chapter in a relationship goes beyond knowing the words or hanging them on the wall.

Instead of waiting to hang love on your wall when you're married, now is the time to put it into practice. Because there is a moment in our lives when we must cross over from childish love to mature love. And the best time to start making that change is today.

As children, we have strong feelings for the people in our lives and think we know what love is. We fantasize about what it would be like to have a family. We absorb images of romantic love from the world around us.

As teenagers, we fantasize about the kiss. Long to hold hands with that special someone in small moments and large. Share our dreams and fears safely with the person who will only tell us we have their full support.

But that view is skewed. It doesn't take into consideration the true challenges and tests that love brings—conflict resolution. An intimate relationship requires a level of maturity that you didn't have to exhibit as a younger person, when all you did was take a date out to the movies and restaurants and hang out with your friends.

Mature love is a choice to keep giving to those committed to you despite their frailties. James 1:4 tells us that we must let perseverance finish its work so that we may be mature and complete, lacking nothing.

Some of your current challenges are designed to create patience and kindness in a life that feels incomplete. Your current life is giving you the opportunity to put away childish envy and selfishness, the need to keep score, the justification for anger, so that there is more room for the spiritual dimension of true love as God intended it. All of these will be needed for the long haul in the relationship you're looking for.

You have to be ready to live out this chapter day in and day out now so that it will shine in the long term.

LET'S PRAY

Lord, help me demonstrate a mature love to everyone in my life now so that it will be developed and perfected when I meet my future spouse. I need to understand what selflessness looks like in me. It sounds impossible, but all things are possible through You. Amen.

Healing Heartbreak

Blessed are those who mourn, for they will be comforted.
MATTHEW 5:4

What happens when you go through a tough breakup? The loss of a romantic relationship isn't often what we think of when we think of grieving, but the grief cycle applies to all losses. The intensity of the grief depends on how much we valued what was lost. You likely don't grieve deeply for the person you exchanged a few texts with before being ghosted. But an exclusive relationship that lasted a few months or more before a painful breakup can trigger grief that can be much more intense than you anticipated.

Friends will often remind you of how horrid the other person was. They will tell you, "Forget them, they weren't right for you anyway," or simply, "Move on! There are plenty of others out there." They may wonder why this breakup has you all twisted up in knots for weeks. Even you might wonder what's wrong with you and why you're not recovering quickly and moving on. You remind yourself that there are worse situations out in the world, but still the painful feelings continue. You might be experiencing a deeper grief that will require time and proper care to recover from even if it doesn't seem to make sense.

David seems to have experienced this cycle as his first child with Bathsheba was dying (2 Samuel 12). David committed adultery with Bathsheba, and then she alerted him that she was pregnant some time later. He arranged for her husband Uriah to be killed in battle and then welcomed her into the palace. Except God knew. The prophet Nathan, through the subterfuge of story, informed the king that the child out of wedlock would not live. Sure enough, when the baby was born, it was weak and sick. David was heartbroken, and he bargained with God through prayer and fasting before accepting God's will once the child had died.

But David's baby was dying, and you're simply experiencing a romantic breakup. You might think the loss is relatively insignificant, but if you are experiencing signs of grief—numbness, disorganization, emotional outbursts, extended shock, crying, lethargy, panic attacks—then it's worth evaluating your current emotional state and taking the time to care for your grief.

It's okay to feel off-kilter. It's okay if you're not as strong as you think you need to be.

Grieving is a normal part of being human. Losses are a part of doing big things. Tears are a part of the healing process. Time heals, but only if you let go and allow the work of healing to happen without minimizing or suppressing your grief.

LET'S PUT IT INTO PRACTICE

Taking the time to heal your grief is a sign not of weakness but of wisdom. Taking the time to participate in counseling, recovery programs, grief support groups, or coaching can help you move through grief and get you back on your feet and back in the game.

Patience = Peace

Whoever is patient has great understanding, but
one who is quick-tempered displays folly.
PROVERBS 14:29

The prophet Jonah preaches repentance to the pagans of Nineveh with the additional promise from God that Nineveh will be destroyed in 40 days.

Except something unexpected happens—they actually repent. God lifts the promise of destruction. Jonah gets angry, telling God he predicted God would lift this destruction when the order to preach first came down from heaven. Still, Jonah can hope God will destroy Nineveh. He waits under a leafy plant a short distance from the city, but then God allows the plant to die, and Jonah wishes he were dead because of the heat. God wonders whether perhaps Jonah should be more concerned about the people in the city than a plant. Seems like Jonah didn't want to enjoy the process of obedience but instead was impatient to get the results he wanted.

Sometimes we can be the dating version of Jonah—impatient to get the results we want without learning what God knows we need in the meantime. Being in a hurry to shed the unwanted state of singleness, to find our perfect match, can create fertile ground for many errors in love. Finding the right person at a time when you both are ready for a deeper commitment of love is more important than finding them when one or both of you aren't properly healed and committed to the other. Otherwise, that's sowing endless troubles for the future. After all, the hurry comes from a deep fear that it won't really happen and we have to force it, that we have to grab the opportunity when it presents itself no matter the circumstances.

While most Westerners consider patience an unnecessary virtue, the renowned sculptor Auguste Rodin said, "Patience is also a form of action." Scripture repeatedly exhorts us to exercise patience, to use it to develop those inner qualities necessary for a healthy mind and attentive spirit. When you exercise patience as part of your deliberate dating strategy, you don't expect every coffee date and swipe right to be the final destination. They're part of a process that can develop you into who God wants you to be.

Be at peace with your time line. God has the perfect path designed for you, and trying to hurry it along is impossible. You will only make your path more difficult. What works is staying present in the moment with a teachable heart. God is wanting to develop more of you during this journey if you're willing. You want to show up at the end with as much of the fruit of the Spirit developed in you as possible. You don't want to show up a grump like Jonah, wondering why you still can't get your way.

LET'S PUT IT INTO PRACTICE

Allow yourself to become more realistic about the length of your dating journey. Create a list of milestones a relationship would need to go through for you to commit. How long do you think it will take once you're pretty sure you found "the One"?

Wisdom Is Not a Four-Letter Word

Since you have asked for this and not for long life or wealth for yourself, nor have asked for the death of your enemies but for discernment in administering justice, I will do what you have asked. I will give you a wise and discerning heart, so that there will never have been anyone like you, nor will there ever be.
1 KINGS 3:11–12

It used to be a comedy cliché: a contemporary individual would climb on hands and knees to the height of a mountain to ask a deep and searching question of a bearded guru sitting cross-legged at the very tip-top. Often the answer came back as a punch line or something nonchalant like "How should I know?"

Whatever the situation, ancient wisdom was often seen as valuable but fluid. Biblical wisdom is no different—instead of instant words with clear direction, it is often something that must be earned through action and experience and then applied over time.

Proverbs, the primary wisdom book in Scripture, is full of nuance, not formulas. It warns of specific scenarios, points in specific directions, offers advice without specific steps, and describes the wise without always telling us how to achieve wisdom. It asks us to rely on godly intuition and then act courageously in a direction that you know is right even if others do it differently. Wisdom in Proverbs is a combination of thoughtfulness and reflection.

King Solomon, son of David, famously prayed for God to give him the wisdom to lead God's people. God granted him that desire—without giving him the immediate steps to act wise. God didn't give him a reading list. God didn't double the size of his brain—"Behold King Solomon, the first man to have sixteen brain lobes!" God simply promised to grant his desire for more wisdom and trusted that Solomon would work to earn it.

King Belshazzar praised the prophet Daniel, saying, "I have heard that the spirit of the gods is in you and that you have insight, intelligence and outstanding wisdom" (Daniel 5:14). What the king didn't seem to know was how many hours Daniel had spent praying, fasting, and studying the Scriptures to earn that praise.

So it is with wisdom today. It is not attainable in three easy steps. It is not a pharmaceutical, and it is not a favorite author or speaker. It is an accumulation of godly desires, smart choices, friends who challenge us to be better, and the intangibles.

Wisdom means your head and heart are connected and your logic and emotions are together in balance. It resists an easy checklist that blinds you to character issues or incompatibilities when a person checks everything on the list. It resists following feelings of love and infatuation while refusing to weigh the serious aspects of a relationship. Wisdom is delayed gratification for a better future—thinking about the future marriage instead of just the immediate feelings of romance.

LET'S PUT IT INTO PRACTICE

The book of Proverbs contains practical wisdom that can help you navigate thorny dating issues. Make a reading plan that will take you through the entire book over the next few months.

Dating Requires Adulting (Autonomy)

*In fact, though by this time you ought to be teachers,
you need someone to teach you the elementary truths of
God's word all over again. You need milk, not solid food!
Anyone who lives on milk, being still an infant, is not
acquainted with the teaching about righteousness. But
solid food is for the mature, who by constant use have
trained themselves to distinguish good from evil.*
HEBREWS 5:12–14

King Solomon was dead. After Solomon had reigned for
40 years and transformed Jerusalem into a city of magnifi-
cence, his son, the 41-year-old Rehoboam, would now reign.
Upon Rehoboam's ascension, the people of Israel told the new ruler
that they would wholly support him if he relaxed the heavy taxation
his father had imposed on everyone to build this city of marvels.

Rehoboam first consulted his father's advisers, men of the previous generation, who agreed with the people. Then he talked to his
friends, who were all feeling their first taste of power. They all agreed
that they would tax the people more heavily than Solomon to show
that they were in charge and couldn't be manipulated. That's what
Rehoboam told the people. The people rebelled, and Rehoboam
watched helplessly as the ten northern tribes split from Judah. The
new king made many mistakes we could all learn from.

The first concerning sign is that Rehoboam did not have any
thoughts of his own about the request about taxation. It's important
to take advice, but you should start with your own thoughts, ideas,
and direction. Then you must be willing to take responsibility for

your decisions. It is critical that anyone hoping to create a success-ful partnership have the emotional maturity to invest time and work into the partnership.

If, like Rehoboam, you don't have the required emotional matu-rity, you won't know what to look for to find a partner who is mature. Some people are able to be autonomous when they are single, but the minute they are in a relationship, they begin to imitate their partner, and they forget who they are.

Some questions to ask yourself before you repeat the mistakes of Rehoboam:

- Do you take responsibility for taking care of your personal needs: Financial, emotional, physical, and mental?

- Do you have core values that you live by—with or without the approval of others? Can you maintain those values even when you are criticized by others?

- Are you able to set boundaries and speak up to protect your core values when they are being violated?

- Can you control your emotions and choose a healthy response in stressful situations?

- Are you dating to find someone to save you from life's challenges, or do you feel confident about problem-solving for yourself?

Taking responsibility for your own life and well-being is the foun-dation of being a true adult. Rehoboam was playing at being king with disastrous consequences. It's important to be sure we are not playing at being adults but walking in maturity.

LET'S PRAY

Lord, sometimes the challenges that come with being an adult can be overwhelming. It's easy to want to run away from being responsible or engaging with difficult tasks and challenging interactions. Help me find the courage to show up mature in everything I do. Amen.

Choosing the Story
We Tell Ourselves

See, I am doing a new thing! Now it springs
up; do you not perceive it?
ISAIAH 43:19

The brain is a complex and powerful organ. It stores millions of memories over our lifetimes. Each memory is stored with multiple dimensions and sensory data—sights, sounds, smells, emotions, meaning, interpretations—that can be recalled in an instant.

This capacity for instant recall can prove to be both a blessing and a curse. When the memory is pleasant, we treasure the nostalgia of a happy past. When the memory is painful, we carry with us images we would rather leave behind.

Another function of the brain is to create meaning out of our lives. It takes all our experiences, and it creates a map from which to make present and future decisions. Again, a blessing and a curse. By default, the brain will try to create safety by focusing on the most painful memories and doing whatever it takes to prevent the pain from happening again.

If you've ever been heartbroken, you know that the excruciating pain of being romantically rejected is one that you would like to avoid at all costs. Sometimes the cost of avoiding future heartbreak is giving up trying again. You may throw yourself into your work or service activities. You may turn down opportunities to meet new people or end potential relationships before they even start.

Because we are human, our perspective of life is limited by our experiences. It is hard to shake off the story that what has happened in the past is the greatest determiner of our future. But God's perspective is infinite and full of unlimited opportunities to create something new. While all we can see is what is in our immediate environment and what we've stored in our memory, God sees the entire planet with all the people, experiences, and opportunities for love and connection that await us. "I make known the end from the beginning, from ancient times, what is still to come" (Isaiah 46:10).

We are often like an impatient child who asks their parent over and over "Are we there yet?" on a long road trip to a fun vacation. But God knows the wonderful end of our dating journey. He sees every step and walks with us as we choose to trust Him.

We may not be able to control the memories that the brain carries with us or the tendency for memories to be triggered involuntarily, but we can choose the story we tell about what is available to us in the present and what awaits us in the future. We can choose to rise above our limited experience and create a story from God's vantage point.

LET'S REFLECT

Stretch yourself to see your dating journey from God's point of view. What do you think He sees? What does He say about your prospects and your ability to find a partner? How does that view compare with yours?

Bringing Failure into the Open

*If we confess our sins, he is faithful and just and will forgive
us our sins and purify us from all unrighteousness.*
1 JOHN 1:9

The dating journey can get messy. If you've been on the journey to find love for any length of time, you have probably made some mistakes. You've done some things that trigger feelings of shame and regret. Maybe you dated the person everyone warned you about, and it turned into a disaster. Maybe you ghosted someone or broke up with them by text. Whatever the situation, your errors are a sure sign that you are human.

Just like a baby falls hundreds of times as they learn to walk, it is impossible to find the relationship you dream of without stumbling along the way. Failure is not a problem; failure is a sign that you are playing the game. The problem arises when you do not properly process failure. The natural tendency is to hide away in guilt and shame.

Hiding causes the problem to fester and shame to grow. We go from making a mistake to feeling as though we are the mistake. Hiding our failures is completely unnecessary, because God is fully aware of them. He knows us better than we know ourselves. He knows that we will need His care, compassion, guidance, and forgiveness every step of the way.

"As a father has compassion on his children, so the Lord has compassion on those who fear him; for he knows how we are formed, he remembers that we are dust" (Psalm 103:13–14).

God has empathy for our humanity. He understands that we are not perfect and can't be. Therefore, He offers His love, kindness, and compassion for every situation we face. The entire story of humanity as written in the Bible is one of people trying and failing over and over and God forgiving them over and over. Moses got angry and struck the rock, David took Uriah's wife, and Paul killed Christians. God offered His love, forgiveness, and restoration to them all.

And He also offers it to you for every situation you have and will face on this potentially challenging dating journey. So instead of hiding away when you fail, connect with God, learn from it, and let it go. There is no reason to compound the mistake by beating yourself up. Using your imperfections against yourself is a surefire way to stop your progress in its tracks.

See every failure as an opportunity to learn, readjust, and get back out there able to do better.

LET'S PUT IT INTO PRACTICE

Make a list of the five to ten dating errors that still make you cringe. As you write, painful emotions may arise. If they do, reread the Scripture of the day, and apply the love, forgiveness, and comfort that God offers to each one of these memories.

Choosing Weird and Wonderful

For John came neither eating nor drinking, and they say,
"He has a demon." The Son of Man came eating and
drinking, and they say, "Here is a glutton and a
drunkard, a friend of tax collectors and sinners."
But wisdom is proved right by her deeds.
MATTHEW 11:18-19

The dating scene is not the place to go for feedback on your lifestyle. It's the fastest way to crush your confidence.

Sarah was messaging with a possible match when the inevitable topic of interests and activities bubbled up. She shared a primary interest that was part of her identity—she loved the outdoors and lived in a yurt during the summer weekends.

The possible match, a man she'd never met, typed, "That's weird. You shouldn't put that on your profile." When the conversation ended, this sharp criticism about something she did out of a deep passion made her second-guess herself, so she got back on her profile and removed the line about the yurt.

Sarah let a complete stranger convince her to delete an essential part of her identity from the view of everyone else. Except that passion is what helped make her who she was. Her perfect partner will be someone who respects her for doing that and would actually be drawn to that activity because it made her different from everyone else. And now that wasn't part of her public dating identity, because she let random criticism crush her confidence.

Personal criticism never stopped raining on Jesus. He was constantly rejected by the religious establishment, but they also rejected John the Baptist, who was the opposite of Jesus. So it didn't matter what each did; they were condemned. Both men made the decision to remain true to themselves no matter what.

Like John and Jesus, you are not for everyone, and you were never meant to be. Not everyone likes every type of food or sport or book. We know this, but we cringe when the criticism stabs us.

Here's a good rule of thumb: 5 to 10 percent of the people you meet are going to be raving fans; 5 to 10 percent of the people will actively dislike you whether or not they have a good reason. Everyone else in the middle will not give you much thought, good or bad.

So don't change yourself based on comments you hear along the dating journey, such as:

"You do what? That's so weird."

"I'm not a fan of that."

"That's nerdy."

"You sound like you're high-maintenance."

"Nobody thinks like that anymore."

"How come every recipe you create in the kitchen takes 17 pots and pans?"

Yes, those words might temporarily deflate your confidence. Yes, those words will feel like personal attacks at times. Yes, those words might actually be true in some aspect or other. But that doesn't mean you shouldn't show the world the person God fearfully and wonderfully made (Psalm 139:14).

Stay true to who you are, and your person will love all of who you are.

LET'S REFLECT

Take some time to think about the things that make you uniquely you: interests, hobbies, likes, dislikes, past experiences, and dreams for the future. Now compare those parts of yourself to the person you present on dates and on your profile. Do they match? It's time to close the gap.

Dating Is an Adventure to (1) Dread or (2) Enjoy. Choose One.

For our light and momentary troubles are achieving
for us an eternal glory that far outweighs them all.
2 CORINTHIANS 4:17

There are two biblical stories to which you can compare your current dating life.

Story 1: Too often we think we are the merchant in the parable of the Good Samaritan, innocently minding our business when we're mugged and attacked by a gang of unsavory dates on Tinder, leaving us bleeding on the side of the road. Then our friends and coworkers want to hear our latest story, but—like the priest and the Levite—they offer no help or comfort. And our story rarely includes a Good Samaritan. It always ends with us bleeding on the side of the road, picking ourselves up off the ground, and stumbling home.

Story 2: Your dating adventure is closer to the Apostle Paul's second missionary journey. He made plans for where he wanted to visit and made lifelong friends along the way, but God also intervened and blocked him from going to Asia Minor and then later unexpectedly sent him to Macedonia, homeland of Alexander the Great. His journey also included being beaten, being thrown in jail with Silas, revival breaking out, and a trip to Athens. Your dating journey will likely be just as unpredictable.

Both stories are apt metaphors for the outlook that dating is an adventure. (You know it's true.) Adventures are both exciting and disappointing, full of joyful surprises and unexpected frustrations. There is no one who would choose the normal archaeology professor who stays on campus and grades papers over Indiana

Jones. Indiana Jones reads the same books as the first professor, but he goes on adventures! So it is with your dating life. Why be complacently single when you could be living a life that is always interesting, though it might dip to the bad or rise to the good.

Tainting your dating life by declaring it drudgery will never allow you to appreciate the stories you can experience and the people you will meet. The Apostle Paul could have complained about his missionary journeys by proclaiming the enemies he made, the long hours on the road, the scars he accumulated, and the utter failure he often faced while preaching. Instead, he chose to measure the effects of his efforts, the joys in the journeys, and the friendships he had accumulated.

So what makes an adventure?

1. The unknown is a regular component of this journey.

2. New friends, acquaintances, and even enemies are accumulated.

3. New experiences unfurl—be it restaurants and food never before tried or visits to previously unknown locales.

4. Dread and excitement are constant companions.

5. There is an agreed-upon end point, though the length of time to get there is not always known.

Adventures don't always turn out the way we expect, but they always enrich our lives—especially those we give to God to direct.

LET'S REFLECT

Write out the ways your dating story is an adventure, not a death march. Look for surprises, unexpected friends (or enemies!), and happy discoveries that have occurred while you're following God's guidance on the pathway to marriage. Write about how this is making your life more interesting and you a better person.

Prayers Answered
Are a Tree of Life

Be joyful in hope, patient in affliction, faithful in prayer.
ROMANS 12:12

So. Much. Praying.

Isaac was praying a lot these days. His father's servant Eliezer was traveling back to Abraham's relatives in Harran to find Isaac a bride. Except they couldn't know for sure their relatives were still living near Harran. They couldn't know whether Eliezer would make the trip east safely, even with his guards. They couldn't know whether there would be eligible women Isaac's age once Eliezer arrived. More important—what if he didn't like her? And even if there was a smart, beautiful woman waiting for Isaac on the other side, there was no guarantee weather or bandits or sandstorms might not hurt them on the return trip.

So. Much. Praying.

And what was taking so long? Eliezer said he'd get there as quickly as possible and head home immediately, but it had been weeks! What was taking him so long? What was taking God so long? Dad wouldn't let Isaac go find her. No, he had to trust Eliezer with that task. Except it wasn't Eliezer's life that was on the line. It was Isaac's life. Dad could've at least let Isaac accompany him to Harran. He was an adult! What would that have hurt? No hurt at all. But here he was—stuck and at the mercy of others. It was agonizing to wait like that, uncertain and emotionally dangling.

So. Much. Praying.

So it is that Scripture tells us that a special—and especially cinematic—evening was at last in store for Isaac.

One evening, Isaac stopped for a drink at a well before wandering out into a field to meditate (or pray). Then, on the horizon, he saw a line of camels silhouetted against the setting sun. Instantly, he recognized Eliezer's colorful turban on the lead rider. And beside him was . . . a woman! Isaac whooped. Then he began dashing across the fields toward the caravan.

So much praying had at last been answered.

Sometimes it can feel awkward praying for a future spouse. It seems desperate. You might worry that praying about finding someone will jinx it. That you will want it too much and that means your request will be denied. Or maybe it feels insignificant. Aren't there more important needs in the world than a future spouse? I mean, have you seen the state of the world today?

Yet Isaac seems to have been praying about his spouse daily despite all of the important duties he was fulfilling. The fact is, God gives you what you pray for when it's a need. Prayer is simply speaking and listening to God on a journey where you need a wise companion. It's not goofy or awkward or desperate. It's wise.

Just ask Isaac. He ended up with one of the most fulfilling marriages in Scripture. But it came after so. Much. Praying.

LET'S PUT IT INTO PRACTICE

Make a commitment to daily prayer for your future spouse and marriage. Write out your prayer and pin it up somewhere in your home where you will see it daily and remember to pray.

The Parable of the Dating Sower: What Kind of Ground Are You?

Sow your seed in the morning, and at evening let your hands not be idle, for you do not know which will succeed, whether this or that, or whether both will do equally well.
ECCLESIASTES 11:6

It's important to remember that you get to choose the approach you want to take for your dating journey. If you don't decide, it gets decided for you, because life isn't static. You will be bombarded with different thoughts, ideas, advice, challenges, situations, and opportunities as you go. God's support, wisdom, and comfort are available for you. How you engage with that assistance is up to you. Will you be wise, or will you be foolish?

Perhaps the best-known parable of Christ is the parable of the Sower (or farmer) who is planting seeds on his property, as detailed in Matthew 13. Along with its spiritual truths, it defines four ways that people tend to choose to engage with outside forces.

"A farmer went out to sow his seed. As he was scattering the seed, some fell along the path, and the birds came and ate it up. Some fell on rocky places . . . It sprang up quickly, because the soil was shallow. But when the sun came up, the plants were scorched, and they withered because they had no root. Other seed fell among thorns, which grew up and choked the plants. Still other seed fell on good soil, where it produced a crop—a hundred, sixty or thirty times what was sown" (Matthew 13:3–8).

We modify this parable into the parable of the dating Sower to help you evaluate your responses to dating:

A dater named Sam went out to date. God dropped wisdom, mercy, and love into Sam's path, but the inspiration and support never took root, because Sam was not consciously making their own decisions. Sam kept changing their mind based on every piece of advice that friends, family, magazines, websites, and TV shows brought their way. Sam acted randomly and impulsively based on what they felt in the moment or each new piece of advice offered.

A dater named Riley went out to date. God dropped wisdom, mercy, and love into Riley's path, but Riley rejected God's inspiration and wisdom when life got hard. Riley complained, "It's not working," "God isn't helping me," and "It's just too hard," and gave up.

A dater named Cory went out to date. God dropped wisdom, mercy, and love into Cory's path, but Cory chose instant gratification, fairy-tale thinking, and unrealistic expectations instead of truly understanding what a healthy, fulfilling relationship looks like.

A dater named Goodie went out to date. God dropped wisdom, mercy, and love into Goodie's path. Goodie chose the healthy principles, thoughts, and actions that lead to a truly fulfilling relationship—even though doing so took patience, effort, and long-suffering to create a yield of 30-fold, 60-fold, and 100-fold. To do that, Goodie continued to take in new information, learn new skills, and engage with God's principles to create real love with the perfect partner.

See yourself in the parable? If not, look again. If so, make the proper corrections necessary to travel your dating journey to success.

LET'S PRAY

Lord, please help me become good ground for everything You've provided for a successful dating journey. Help me see the gifts and resources I already have inside myself and the opportunities You continue to put along my path to give me success. Amen.

Acknowledgments

Thank you to Dr. Chavonne Perotte for encouraging us to take on this project and to our editor, Chloe Moffett, for her feedback and support. The late Pastor Dave Roberson of the Family Prayer Center in Tulsa, Oklahoma, must also be included for his steady emphasis on going beyond the obvious surface truths of Scripture to connect with the gems available from a deeper reading.

About the Authors

Kent and Sade Curry live in the Saint Louis, Missouri, metropolitan area and have six children in their blended family. Sade is a life and relationship coach who works with divorced women to help them rebuild their lives, achieve their goals, and get married again. Kent is a Bible teacher who also speaks at regional and national conferences, sharing his passions for student ministries, biblical application, and recovery work. Together they facilitate relationship workshops for single people, divorced individuals, and remarried couples who want to create loving, connected, and healthy relationships.